How to Increase Your Personal Wealth

How to Increase Your Personal Wealth

Peter Cutler, Ph.D

Thorsons
An Imprint of HarperCollins*Publishers*

Thorsons
An Imprint of HarperCollins*Publishers*
77-85 Fulham Palace Road,
Hammersmith, London W6 8JB

Published by Thorsons 1992
10 9 8 7 6 5 4 3 2 1

A catalogue record for this book
is available from the British Library

ISBN 0 7225 2550 8

Typeset by Harper Phototypesetters Limited,
Northampton, England
Printed in Great Britain by
Mackays of Chatham, Kent

Contents

To Janet and Norman, with much love
and thanks for all your kindness.

CHAPTER 1

The Rewards Open to You

Would *you* like to be wealthy? Just think of the advantages of having ready money!

Let your imagination roam free for a moment: You own your house outright – there are no more monthly mortgage payments to make. You drive the car that you really want, not just the one that you think you can afford. Perhaps you send your children to private school. You enjoy – permanently – that comfortable 'money in the bank feeling'. You regularly travel abroad. You have no worries about having enough income in old age. In short, you are financially independent.

Is this just a daydream, some imaginary lane to wander pleasantly along amid the bustle of everyday worries? Or is it something offered only to the chosen few who enjoy luck or some special talent? The answer, fortunately, is a resounding No! All of these delights are open to any person, even if on an average income or less. This is so for one simple reason. *As long as you have an income, of whatever level, you have the opportunity to build capital.*

Other than the fact that you need an income, of whatever size, all that must now be added is a little planning, some willingness to learn and explore new information, and a modest amount of determination. The message of this book is straightforward. Any person, on an average salary or even less, can achieve 'wealth' – by which is meant independent financial means – just by defining his or her objectives and establishing a basic programme of saving and investment in order to achieve them.

If this seems hard to believe, just consider this fact. If you earn a salary of £12,000, and this salary grows at only 8 per cent a year over a working lifetime, by the time you retire, a total of £4 million will have passed through your hands! If you then take only 10 per cent of this salary and invest it at a rate of 12 per cent annually, you will have accumulated a lump sum worth, in today's money, over £300,000 over the same period.

Of course, you can do a lot better than this if you decide to earn more and save more. And you don't have to wait until you retire to enjoy the rewards! I say *decide*, because this is entirely in your hands. You can start saving right now and you can begin to plan ways of increasing your income. You don't have to be a financial wizard to do this – you just need to be clear about your objectives.

But, you might protest, I am already finding it difficult to make ends meet! By the end of the month there is nothing left of my pay. This is usually the case, which is why you deduct the money for your savings plan from your salary automatically at the *beginning* of the month. This amounts to a form of tax – but one entirely for your own benefit! Later we will explore practical methods of taking control of your finances and eliminating waste, so that you are able to save painlessly.

Living in the Real World

What if you decide *not* to save and invest a proportion of your income? Unfortunately, we live in a world where the divide between those who have money and those who do not is increasing. In this highly competitive age the implications of this gap are becoming more important. Whether we like it or not, the State is no longer able to guarantee full employment, a substantial index-linked pension, comprehensive welfare benefits, or prompt medical treatment. For those of us reared on the post-war welfare system this may be something of a shock. None the less, it is a fact of modern life.

Politicians promise a great deal, whatever their party, but are increasingly unable to deliver benefits which depend upon a flourishing economy, strong tax revenues, and accelerating government spending. This is a problem not confined to our own society, but is common to many other European and North American countries which would otherwise be considered rich. Welfare expenditures become further constrained when economies are in recession, or even in a state of prolonged economic slump. This spectre, previously dismissed as fantasy and a long-forgotten nightmare of the distant 1930s, has returned to haunt us in the 1990s.

At the same time, we have experienced the development of opportunities available to the ordinary person which were simply unthinkable in our grandparents' time. The general availability of specialist education and training has meant that strong-willed people have been able to catapult themselves to prosperity by gaining and marketing sales-worthy skills. The children of the unskilled and semi-skilled working classes have in increasing numbers reached the heights of business and the professions. Each has done so by exploiting his or her particular talents, and by developing the technical skills required along the way. British society is not as closed as it once was, although it is certainly more competitive. Opportunities for go-getting individuals have never been greater.

The fact that you are reading this book means you have a strong desire to improve your lot in life. You will have come to understand that it is entirely up to you to make your way in the world. Perhaps you have already begun to enjoy a satisfactory career, or perhaps you are coming to a decision about just what it is you want out of life. Either way, you will benefit from reviewing your personal finances. Following a short 'orientation course' which will help you to decide exactly where you want to go, we shall embark on a review of the investment options that will help you get there.

Whom Would You Prefer to Be?

The Western world can be said to contain three types of people. There are those who live on the breadline, whether or not they have a job. They may feel that it is up to 'someone', such as their employer or the Government, to improve their lot in life. Of course it is true that they have a right to be happy and to enjoy expressing their talents, but this must come from within and be the result of their own efforts, it cannot be counted upon to be granted externally by an employer or the government.

The second type is made up of those who are reasonably happy with their work, and are busy making money, but who are spending it just as fast as they can. In fact they are probably overspending, and are going into debt. These people have the potential to be independently wealthy, but they never will be until they free themselves of their spendthrift attitude. This can easily be done, however, as I have already explained in my previous book, *Get Out of Debt and Prosper*.

The third type of person is independent. People of this type know what they want to achieve in life, set out purposefully to get it, and systematically save and invest a proportion of their income as an integral part of their plan to succeed. The exciting thing is that what they are doing is very powerful; it has a cumulative and accelerating effect. Consequently, these individuals appear to succeed almost effortlessly.

In fact, what successful individuals do takes effort, applied daily in a focused and intelligent fashion. But this 'effort' is more in the nature of a habit, and does not require painful sacrifice. On the contrary, it increases personal energy and general levels of success.

Questionnaire

At this point, it is worth embarking on some serious self-examination. This will help you to decide where you are, and where you want to be. Take a few minutes to complete this questionnaire, and think about the results.

1. Write down your income, and think about it for a minute. Is it enough for your needs? How much do you think you could increase it by in the coming year?
    - a. Nothing (0 points)
    - b. By 10 – 20 per cent or so (2 points)
    - c. By 30 per cent or more (3 points)
    - d. By 50 per cent or more (5 points)
2. Do you enjoy your job?
    - a. I hate it (0 points)
    - b. Not much, but it's a living (1 point)
    - c. I like my job, but would like to earn more (3 points)
    - d. I love it, and wouldn't do anything else (5 points)
3. Are you unemployed? If so, how are you going about finding other jobs?
    - a. I use the job centre and reply to advertisements (2 points)
    - b. I'm retraining to work in a different field (4 points)
    - c. I've basically given up looking because it's hopeless (0 points)
    - d. I am actively looking for work, using both formal and informal contacts (5 points)
4. If you are buying a house on a mortgage, have you considered reducing the size of the loan or repaying it early?
    - a. I don't consider it feasible (0 points)
    - b. I would be willing to increase the loan repayments (3 points)
5. If you are renting a home, have you thought about buying one?
    - a. I don't think I could possibly afford it (0 points)
    - b. I am already saving for a deposit (5 points)
6. Does your bank current account pay interest?
    - a. Yes (3 points)
    - b. No (0 points)
7. How do you clear the balance of your credit cards?
    - a. In full and on time every month (5 points)
    - b. I only pay the minimum (1 point)
    - c. I pay varying amounts depending upon the state of my finances (3 points)
8. Do you think you can make savings on your monthly expenditure?
    - a. I don't see how it is possible (0 points)

✓b. I'm already spending as little as possible (2 points)

   c. Yes, there is always room for improvement (3 points)

9. When did you last fill in a tax return form?

   a. I have never asked for one (0 points)

✓b. I fill one in every year (3 points)

10. Do you own any shares?

   a. No, I don't know enough about them (0 points)

✓b. Yes, I have some of the privatisation stocks (2 points)

   c. Yes, I invest in shares regularly (3 points)

   d. No, I don't think it is the right time to buy shares (3 points)

11. Have you any National Savings certificates?

✓a. No, I don't know much about them (0 points)

   b. Yes, just one type of scheme (2 points)

   c. Yes, more than one scheme (4 points)

12. Do you own any gilts or gilt unit trusts?

✓a. No, I don't know what they are (0 points)

   b. Yes, I have already added these to my portfolio (3 points)

13. Do you have life insurance?

✓a. Yes, I am adequately covered (3 points)

   b. I rely only on my employer's scheme (1 point)

   c. I haven't bothered because I have no dependents (3 points)

   d. I have dependents but I am not covered (0 points)

14. Have you made a will?

   a. No, I don't think I need one (1 point)

✓b. I intend to make one within the next 12 months (2 points)

   c. My will is completed and is up to date (5 points)

15. Do you deal in futures or traded options markets?

✓a. No, I don't know anything about them (1 point)

   b. I wouldn't like to, it's too dangerous (3 points)

   c. I tried it once but got wiped out (3 points)

   d. I deal regularly, in a cautious way (5 points)

16. Have you thought hard about what you want out of life and how to get it?

✓a. I haven't really given it much thought (0 points)

   b. I used to have big plans, but it's hard enough just to get by (2 points)

   c. I know exactly where I want to go and how to get there (5 points)

17. Do you work at a part-time occupation?

✓a. No, I don't think I need to (2 points)

   b. I'd like to but I don't have the time (1 point)

   c. I'd like to but there are no opportunities (1 point)

   d. Yes, I work regularly to earn extra cash (5 points)

18. If you answered yes to the above, what do you do with the money?

   a. Spend it all on household expenses (2 points)
   b. Spend it on holidays and treats (3 points)
   c. Save some and spend some (4 points)
   d. Save most or all of it (5 points)
19. Are you studying to improve your career prospects?
   ✓a. No, I don't need to (1 point)
   b. I have enough qualifications, but I try to keep up to date with developments (3 points)
   c. Yes, I am taking recognized courses in my field (5 points)
   d. Yes, I am studying to change my occupation (5 points)
20. Do you read much about current economic affairs?
   a. No, I don't understand any of it (0 points)
   b. I don't find it very interesting (1 point)
   c. Yes, I try to keep up, but it is very confusing (2 points)
   ✓d. Yes, I try hard to keep up to date (3 points)

Scoring

Now add up your scores. Let's see how you have done.

1 - 15 You don't seem to be very confident at the moment. Perhaps you have been having a hard time generally. If things are this bad, they can only get better!

16 - 30 Already you are improving your prospects, but there is quite a lot to work on. It's time to make a start on your weaker points.

31 - 45 You are off to a good start. Think hard about what aspects of your financial life could be improved upon. Probably you could tighten up a bit on savings, and make greater efforts to invest.

45 or more You are certainly very well organized and financially aware. If this is the case you are well on the way to independent financial status. Keep up the good work!

Success Will Be Yours!

Much has been written about the secrets of success. A lot of good advice has been given, and I have listed some useful references in the Appendix. If you haven't read some of the classic works on the subject then I strongly recommend that you get hold of copies. The 'secrets' expounded in these books are in fact just ancient common-sense truths of which we often need to be reminded.

This book does not try to duplicate these works. I am starting out with the assumption that you want to be successful, and already recognize that in addition to orientating your life to the kind of work that you like to do, and pursuing a vigorous career plan to help you to do it, that you will want to accumulate additional financial wealth within a reasonable length of time but without taking on excessive risks. In chapter 2 we will quickly run through the planning process to set you on the right road to wealth. For now, we shall concentrate on the main message of this book, which bears repeating:

The ordinary person, no matter how low his or her salary, can accumulate wealth through saving and investing a proportion of income every month.

Unfortunately, for many people the act of saving seems to be beyond the bounds of possibility, while investment seems to be a subject which is best left only to experts, who can understand all the jargon and complexities of the financial markets.

My argument is that the opposite is true. Saving is not really difficult; and neither is investment. What is required is a firm objective, independence of mind, and the basic intelligence which we all possess. The jargon is used by the so-called experts – many of whom are simply highly-paid salespeople earning large commissions – to mystify the general public. They may well have little overall knowledge of finance, and even less of economics.

These 'experts' don't necessarily want investment to be accessible to you, as if it is then there will be little or no profit in it for them.

What This Book Will Do For You

This book has been written, in plain English and avoiding jargon where possible (and explaining terms fully where it is not), to help you do the following:

- Understand the benefits of successful saving and investment
- Define your investment objectives
- Identify where savings can be made and income increased in order to help you find the money to invest
- Understand basic economic cycles, so as to guide your major investment decisions
- Improve your day-to-day cash management
- Find out what home mortgage to take, and how to repay it quickly
- Identify efficient pension and life assurance plans
- Understand the role of bonds in your investment portfolio
- Discover the best value financial vehicles for stock-market investment
- Decide when and how to buy gold for maximum profit
- Learn how to speculate without losing your shirt
- Minimize your tax bills to maximize your savings
- Identify investment opportunities in the present decade and beyond
- Manage your retirement and minimize the burden of inheritance tax

My aim is to show you that investment is not a difficult subject to comprehend. The degree of interest you take in it will probably depend upon the amount you have invested and on your own fascination for markets. To begin with you will probably need to take a couple of afternoons or evenings to review your situation and to plan your future. After that you will want to spend an hour or two every month or so monitoring your progress.

As you grow more knowledgeable and financially aware you will read newspapers and watch TV with new eyes, weighing up the investment implications of the news and current affairs. Investing is endlessly fascinating, and potentially very profitable. Remember that you do not have to achieve spectacular returns or get rich quickly. You just have to invest patiently and intelligently to get rich steadily. Your first 10-year, £50,000 nest-egg could be only £25 a week away!

Key Points

- At least £4 million is likely to pass through your hands in your lifetime. Make sure some of it stays with you!
- You do not have to take spectacular risks to get wealthy. Simply save 10 per cent of your income each month and invest it carefully.
- It is up to you to decide whether you want wealth or poverty.
- It takes only a minimum amount of effort to save and invest.
- The time to start your savings programme is *now*.

CHAPTER 2

Taking Control of Your Finances

Before springing into action and rushing off to put your hard-earned cash into all and sundry investments, it is important to take stock of where you are now and where you want to be in the future. This is particularly the case if you are currently finding it hard to manage your day-to-day affairs. You must work out a plan that suits your individual needs and allows you to release funds for investment. In this chapter we shall consider how you can take control of your financial affairs by establishing your goals and drawing up a realistic timetable for achieving them.

Deciding to Build Your Wealth

The starting point is, of course, desire. If you do not have the desire to achieve wealth from a modest income then you will not find the impetus to embark on a wealth-creation programme. Neither will you find the self-discipline required to stay on track.

However, it is not particularly difficult to save and invest. It is simply a habit, like any other. Your worst enemy at the start is procrastination. The longer you wait the less money you will make. So it is vital you set aside the time to plan your future *now*.

The Rewards of Saving and Investment

If you have read my previous book, you will already be aware of the amazing power of compound interest. This power, like any other, can be constructive or destructive. If you are in serious debt, the daily accumulation of compound interest on the outstanding balances will turn a debt molehill into a mountain – unless you arrest and reverse the process, which *Get Out of Debt and Prosper* tells you in detail how to do. If however you are in a position to save money on a weekly or monthly basis, then the daily accumulation of compound interest will soon transform into a mighty heap of money. The rate at which it grows obviously depends upon the rate of interest achieved. However, we can take a fairly conservative example, at interest rates currently achievable, in order to make the point:

Table 1: Growth of Monthly Savings over Different Periods, at a Compound Annual Interest Rate of 10% Net

Years	£100	£200	£300	£400	£500
		Amount Saved per Month:			
5	9,068	18,136	27,205	36,273	45,341
10	27,966	55,931	83,897	111,863	139,829
15	67,786	135,573	203,359	271,145	338,932
20	151,695	303,391	455,086	606,782	758,477
25	328,507	657,015	985,522	1,314,029	1,642,537

There are a number of interesting points to be made about Table 1. The first is that with compound interest, the growth of money saved <u>accelerates over time</u>. The sooner you can start to save, and the longer you can hold the sums saved at a given rate of interest, the greater will be the proportionate benefit. For example, if you save £100 per month for five years, the £6,000 cash you have saved will grow by over 50 per cent by the end of that period, adding £3,068 to your cash savings. Add another £6,000 by saving £100 per month over the next five-year period, and interest on the total sum will add a further £12,898 to your first five years' savings. The interest on the total grows much quicker than you might at first imagine.

A second point is that if you can manage to double or treble your <u>monthly savings</u>, the final benefits will be <u>substantially increased</u>. For example, over a 20-year period, every extra £100 you can save each month translates into over £150,000 extra over the period. In fact, <u>if you could save £500 per month for a total of 22 years at an</u> average interest rate of 10 per cent, <u>you would become a millionaire</u>.

A third point is that this table assumes that you keep the monthly rate of savings constant. In reality, you would probably be able and willing to increase it on an <u>annual or semi-annual basis</u> in line with increases in your income, thereby further accelerating the growth rate of the money saved. In Table 2 we see what effect this can have. This time we are assuming annual savings of £1,000, which are increased each year by 10 per cent. We will also assume a higher interest rate, say 20 per cent.

Table 2 shows that given these assumptions you will accumulate over £40,000 after only 10 years. This period has been chosen as one which most people can relate to – it is not that long a time to

Table 2: Growth of £1,000 Increased Annually by 10%; at an Interest Rate of 20% net

End of Year	Amount Accumulated
1	£ 1,200
2	£ 2,760
3	£ 4,644
4	£ 7,038
5	£10,057
6	£13,842
7	£18,560
8	£24,418
9	£31,661
10	£40,589

wait for the benefits this money would bring.

Furthermore, the money is invested at a rate of return which is a reasonable target. Careful selection of financial funds which suit the general economic climate, are well-run and are not subject to high management charges should achieve this result. Some years may not be as profitable as others, but good years will make up for bad ones. Well-run pension funds, for example, would consider such a rate of return to be feasible, without unduly sacrificing prudence.

Of course, it is up to you to decide how much you feel able to save annually. For some people, £100 a month will seem difficult to find, although in the next chapter we shall identify ways of finding it even within existing incomes. For others, £500 a month will be a reasonable target. Whatever your circumstances, it is important to stop and think about the benefits of a planned savings scheme.

Consider the difference it would make to your financial future if within 10 year's time you could have between £40,500 and £202,945 to play with, depending upon whether you can save £19 a week or £96 a week, increased at 20 per cent annually, as in Table 2. And think of the difference it would make to your future if you do *not* begin to save and invest that money. The difference between a dream house, dream holidays, dream car and dream future – and an ordinary, boring, everyday standard of living, which is the fate of those who can't be bothered to make the effort.

Do It Now!

The time to start planning your financial future is right now. The results I have indicated above are achievable, but they do require a little thought and planning. You cannot blindly hand over your financial future to some faceless corporation and hope that everything will work out right. You cannot depend upon the advice of some salesperson or broker who is interested only a commission or sales targets. You cannot ignore the powerful tides of economic behaviour, which can make you or break you. You cannot depend upon the received wisdom of the crowd, and do what everybody else is doing, if you wish to achieve superior investment returns.

It is up to you to discover where the best value is and what to invest in, when to be bold and when to be cautious. After all, it is your hard-earned money, and it is up to you to protect it and nurture it. Nobody will be as concerned about your money as you are, despite pleas to the contrary from all the vested interests who are trying to get their hands on it.

Where You Want to Be

It is amazing how few people have a plan for living. Some people have made a will – a plan for dying – but they have never bothered to direct their lives with as much enthusiasm. It would not be an exaggeration to observe that the majority of people live from day to day much of the time. This is not to say that they don't wish for things – people do this all the time, saying: 'I wish I could afford to live in a bigger house' or 'I wish I had a better job'. Wishing is fine, but it is only turned into concrete fact by planning, determination and effort.

I don't want you to get the impression that I am advocating a life of unremitting toil. Far from it – your goal in life should be to enjoy the present as well as plan for the future. Unfortunately, if you don't get on with planning for the future you are unlikely to enjoy the present quite as much, because you won't have established the necessary surpluses of time and of money. It requires little effort to establish a plan, and this effort is paid off so well that you gain a great deal more energy and efficiency, and are able to accomplish much more than before without sacrificing your quality of life.

I should add that before we discovered this fact my wife and I like many other people wasted a lot of time and got very little done. By applying the principles of planning time and money we achieved major breakthroughs in our personal lives. Within a year, for example, we had both started new careers. The following year we managed to holiday abroad twice, in addition to enjoying several breaks in the UK. At the same time, my wife studied psychology and I completed my third book. We also managed to invest substantial sums in addition to our existing holdings.

Now, I would not say that we were out of the ordinary, we are both working people with regular jobs in addition to our other activities. But I would say that this schedule of activities would not have been possible without clear personal goals and efficient planning.

The results of establishing a plan for living, as those who have done so will enthusiastically agree, are extraordinarily powerful. Not only do you know exactly where you want to go, but you start getting there fast. Your job has a purpose beyond keeping you clothed and fed. You and your partner develop a more harmonious relationship because you have common goals. If you have children they will benefit both materially and emotionally. Your career will take off like a rocket, or else you will find yourself switching to a job and career more to your liking. All of these things will go on regardless of economic circumstances, because you will have what the psychologists call 'inner direction'.

Establishing Your Goals

The first thing to do is to sit down with a blank sheet of paper and write down all the things you would like to do in life – no matter how outlandish they might seem or how divorced they might be from your present circumstances. This is your 'wish list'. Keep it and add to it whenever you like. It will provide you with lots of material for future objectives.

The next step is to select from the list those wishes which are the most important to you at present. Some of them will be short-term objectives, such as 'buy a car', while others will be medium- to long-term, such as 'own a country house' or 'visit Australia'. You should draw up a short-list of not more than a dozen wishes at a time, which you will concentrate on. These will become your immediate goals.

You can use the practice of goal-setting on any time basis – daily, weekly, monthly, annually, five-yearly or lifetime. It is entirely up to you what you consider to be your most meaningful objectives. It is important, however, that you really want them rather than merely wish for them. Otherwise you will not summon up the energy to go after them. Also, if you have a partner, you will want to ensure that your goals are harmonious. If you are both driving towards a joint goal – such as buying a substantial home – then the dream will have twice as much chance of becoming reality.

Once you have thought hard about your goals and prioritized them, you should write them down in a place where you can refer to them frequently. It is important that you do so on at least a daily basis. If mentally you are thinking constantly about what you want to achieve, then you are pouring energy into that goal, and it will soon become reality. Through daily referrals your desire for the goal will also be strengthened, which will enable you to achieve it that much more quickly.

It is also important that you stay on track, and do not deviate as a result of day-to-day pressures. The more you concentrate on your goals, the more circumstances will bend to your will and allow you to achieve them. It will also help if you visualize these future achievements frequently. The clearer your vision, the easier it will be to achieve your aims. Your mind will find it easier to focus on crystal-clear objectives.

Where Are You Now?

Having established your goals, which will require financing, you will now need to consider your personal financial circumstances. To do this, you will need to consider yourself almost as a small business, and draw up a balance sheet of your assets and liabilities. Rest assured – you will probably find out that you are already richer than you think you are!

It will be helpful if you complete the following questionnaire so that you can put together a complete picture of your net worth – that is, the sum of your assets minus your liabilities. We shall begin with your assets (see Table 3).

Table 3: Your Assets

1. Home   a. Amount of outstanding mortgage:
                   b. Realistic current valuation:
                   c. Net value (b minus a):
2. Car   Realistic value
3. Valuables   Jewellery, etc. at insurance valuation
                   White goods at market prices
4. Pension   Current value of the fund
5. Life Assurance Surrender value of any policies
6. Savings   Building Society deposits
                   (+ accrued interest)
                   Bank deposits
                   Current value of National Savings certificates
7. Investments   Market value of share certificates
                   Market value of unit trusts at bid price
                   Market value of any other investments

There are a few points to bear in mind when making calculations of the worth of your assets. The first is that your valuations must be realistic. For example, for houses it is suggested that you take the 'book price', which is the valuation commonly given for similar houses in your area, or the average of valuations made by estate agents, and deduct up to 10 per cent, depending on the state of the market. If the market is depressed, then this will allow for a realistic price, which may be below the asking price. If the market is buoyant in your area, then you can stick to the book price.

The same applies to cars. The book price can be ascertained from one of the price guides obtainable from newsagents. Be realistic in assessing the condition of your car, and deduct 10 per cent if the market is depressed.

Jewellery and household goods such as TVs, radios, stereos, refrigerators and washing machines will be valued conservatively. Consult the pages of your local newspaper to find out at what price similar goods are being sold for in your area. You will find that these belongings can only be valued at a third or so of their buying prices. Of course, I am not suggesting that you go out and sell them, simply that you obtain a realistic valuation. Jewellery, for example, may only be worth its gold, silver or precious metals content rather than the intrinsic value of its design or craftsmanship.

If you have a personal pension fund of the 'with-profits' type, its value will equal that given in the last annual statement from the company, plus any accrued contributions, plus an estimate of fund growth based on average yearly performance. If it is of the unit-linked type, then you can calculate its value by multiplying the number of units you currently hold by the value of the units given in the financial press. The value of life assurance should be calculated by contacting the company that issues it and asking for a quote as to its 'surrender value'. This may be less than the value of the accrued contributions, depending upon the length of time over which you have held the policy, and the rules applied by the company.

The valuation of building society deposits should include accrued interest if this is paid on an annual or semi-annual basis and has not recently been added to the account. The same holds true for bank deposits, unless interest is added monthly, in which case you can just consult your latest statement.

The market value of shares and unit trust certificates can be calculated simply by multiplying the bid price (selling price) quoted in the financial press by the number of shares or units that you hold. Other investments, such as National Savings certificates, should be calculated at their value should you have to cash them in now rather than hold them to maturity.

Your Liabilities

It is now necessary to deduct liabilities (apart from your mortgage, which has already been taken into account in the calculation above) from the total of a valuation of your assets. These would include the following:

- Credit Card Debt: Each type of card, current total due as of the last statement, plus any extra purchases
- Store Debt: Outstanding balance on storecards or accounts
- Bank Loans: Outstanding amount due (monthly payment × number of payments to the end of the term)
- Bank revolving loan account: Total currently outstanding
- Overdraft: Amount currently outstanding
- Hire Purchase Agreements: Monthly payment × the number of months to the end of the term
- Other loans: Any other loans you may have outstanding, including ones made to you on a personal basis by friends or relatives

Your list of possible liabilities may be quite long, but hopefully it will not outweigh your assets. If it does, don't worry. You will be able to prioritize the repayment of non-essential debts as a means of rapidly freeing up extra cash for investment. I shall have more to say on this topic in chapter 3.

The above exercise might seem to be a bit tedious, but nevertheless it is well worth doing to ascertain the true position of your assets and liabilities. It is quite probable that you are worth more than you first thought, which is a good start for any savings and investment programme.

Reaching Your Goals

Having completed the tasks of defining your goals and assessing your means, you will now know where you are starting from and where you want to go. These are the two key reference points on your personal map. Very few people actually give considered thought to either of these reference points. What you have done has already put you firmly on the path to achieving your objectives.

Your final planning task is to estimate the time it will take you to reach your large and small objectives. This will depend upon a number of factors, including your ambition, your current income, and your self-image. It should be stressed here that the last factor is potentially the most limiting. Many people seem to believe that they are not capable of achieving very much in life, so they automatically put severe limits on their potential for achievement.

Assuming that you have set goals which are reasonably ambitious but achievable according to your own self-confidence, you will also need to set time limits for their achievement. Time limits are required to prevent your goals from slipping back into the never-never land of wishes. We can set time limits by breaking up each goal into smaller components. For example, suppose you are determined to buy a house, and need to raise a deposit of £10,000. You might decide that this will take you three years, given a little bit of effort and dedication. So you might set the steps to the goal as follows:

1. Year 1: Save £2,000 + interest @ 14% = £2,280
2. Year 2: Save £2,600 + £2,280 + interest @ 14% = £5,563
3. Year 3: Save £3,250 + £5,563 + interest @ 14% = £10,047

The interest rate given in this example is fairly conservative, and with this rate of return you will need to increase your savings by around 27 per cent a year in order to reach your goal.

From this annual goal you would be able to estimate the amount of monthly savings required to reach it, for example:

1. Year 1: £167
2. Year 2: £217
3. Year 3: £271

The figures given in this example may seem either a lot to you or an easy target, depending upon your present circumstances. If they seem like a lot, then you might want to consider ways of increasing your earnings or reducing your outgoings in order to meet them. We shall consider how you might do this in chapter 3.

Aim High!

There is no doubt that it is desire, rather than exceptional intelligence or ability, that is the most important element in any wealth-creation programme. When desire is allied to careful planning and only a little extra effort, the results are marvellous to behold. The stronger your desire and more serious your effort, the more extraordinary are your results.

When you consider how few people make that little extra effort to plan their future and to work that little bit harder and more intelligently to get there, then you will begin to realize that by being in the minority – which I would estimate to be one in a hundred – you already have a head start.

If you are still suffering from disbelief at this point, perhaps feeling burdened with debt, family responsibilities, or what you perceive to be a dead-end job paying little, then read on. In the next chapter we shall address the apparent 'problem' of finding the extra money for saving and investment. The problem contains within it the seeds of its own solution.

Key Points

- The starting point for any wealth-building programme is desire. Don't be afraid to be ambitious!

- It is vital to define exactly where you want to go. Write down your goals in detail and refer to them daily.

- Already you will own assets, and it is worth taking the time to discover exactly what these amount to, once your liabilities have been taken into account.

- Compound interest is the saver's best friend, accelerating the growth of interest payments over time.

- Set time limits on your objectives, and break them down into smaller components so that you can see clearly how they can be achieved. Once the route is clearly defined, the objective will soon become a reality.

CHAPTER 3

Finding the Money

In this chapter we shall identify ways in which you can find the extra cash with which to save and invest.

In my previous book, *Get Out of Debt and Prosper*, I argued that if you start seeing problems as opportunities rather than hoping that they will go away, then you will find the courage to tackle them and soon they will be transformed into milestones on your personal route to self-fulfilment.

For many people the problem of finding the money with which to begin a savings and investment programme seems to be insurmountable. However, we can turn this problem on its head and see it as an opportunity. This opportunity comes in three parts:

1. getting the savings habit;
2. reducing your expenditure; and
3. increasing your income.

All of these objectives are easily obtainable for a motivated person, of whatever age, skills or qualifications.

Getting the Savings Habit

One of the seemingly most difficult things to do at first, but which quickly becomes a habit, is to put away a proportion of your pay each week or month *as soon as you receive it*. This discipline gives you no chance to rush out and spend all your wages straight away. The money should go into an account which is not easily accessible. One of the bank or building society high-interest accounts will suffice, particularly if it requires 30 days' notice prior to retrieving the cash without penalty. This money is for investment, and should not be broken into for the purposes of everyday consumption.

You may at this point argue that it is simply impossible for you to do this, as your outgoings regularly exceed your income. Nevertheless, I would suggest that you set about doing it now. You will find that you will simply adjust to your new financial regime, as you would if the Government suddenly raised taxes, or if your employer were to cut your wages. Perhaps you should consider the money as a tax on yourself, which Schwartz has aptly called a 'financial freedom tax' (see the Appendix). Of course, the advantage of such a tax is that its benefits all accrue to you, and not to the Government.

You may also be wondering about how much you should attempt to save. I would recommend that you put away at least ten per cent of your net (after-tax) income, or, preferably, ten per cent of your gross (before-tax) income. This would soon build up to a respectable sum of money.

To some extent your expenditure will automatically adjust to this new tax. However you can help the process along, and even find more room for saving, by reducing your outgoings.

Reducing Your Expenditure

There are of course a great many things that we spend money on. Some are essentials, such as the mortgage or rent, fuel bills, food and clothing, etc. Many are not exactly essentials, but we have come to consider them so, such as the expenses associated with running a car. And some are luxuries, which we really could do without.

The secret of reducing your outgoings is to review your overall expenditure and cut out those inessentials which you really could do away with, *without sacrificing your quality of life*. I am not suggesting that you give up holidays, sports, or going to the pub or the cinema. I am suggesting that you review carefully your expenditure on these items, and consider where savings might be made with little hardship. For example, why not forgo an evening down the pub for an evening planning your finances? The latter will help you get richer, the former poorer. Similarly, if you spend a small fortune on clothes, you may find it more cost-effective to buy quality clothing less often.

Apart from these obvious sources of budgeting, there are sources of expenditure that are more 'hidden' and that you may wish to reduce. For example, if you have a sweet tooth, you may find that you are spending a couple of hundred pounds a year on sweets and chocolate. If you are a smoker this bill might be considerably higher – more like four or five hundred pounds a year for a moderate smoker. You may not want to give up these indulgences, but on the other hand you might find the incentive to cut down.

Table 4: Hidden Sources of Savings for Wealth-building

Mortgage: Have you got a competitive interest rate? Check your position (see chapter 7) and switch if possible.

Rent: Is it worth moving to a cheaper area? Could you share and reduce your outgoings? Is it cheaper or better value to buy?

Credit cards: Are you allowing interest payments to pile up on outstanding balances? Stop using them and pay off the backlog as soon as possible.

Life assurance: Are you getting the best deal? Switch to term insurance and shop around. See chapter 8.

Utilities: Can you economize more on gas, electricity, oil or coal? Turn down the central heating thermostat. Are you using the phone effectively? Insist on making calls at cheaper rates only, or switch to Mercury to make savings on trunk calls.

Food: Are you buying effectively? Think about buying in bulk, and use street markets more often. Would a freezer save you money? Cut out some of the fattening treats (which tend to cost more) and eat more of the healthy basics. Particularly in reference to *lunches*: If there is a subsidized canteen at work, make sure you use it. If not, why not take sandwiches? Stay away from eating out.

Drink: Watch the alcohol bill carefully, this can be a major source of overspending. If you drink lots of mineral water, a good water filter will save you money. Cut down the soft-drinks bill by using concentrates rather than ready-mixed.

Clothes: Plan your spending and buy better quality clothes less often. Take advantage of seasonal sales.

Transport: Investigate the best off-peak and season ticket deals.

Car: If you don't use it much, could you dispense with it altogether? If you do use it a lot, could you switch to a more economical model? Do your own servicing and simple repairs – go on a course if you need to learn how. Shop around and compare prices for garage repairs.

Holidays: Have a no-frills break closer to home rather than that expensive exotic foreign holiday.

TV and video: If you are renting, think about buying on interest-free credit or lease-purchase, it is probably far cheaper.

Periodicals: Newspapers and magazines can cost a great deal over a year. Reduce your reading to essentials, when you have the time. Use office copies and libraries more.

Sports and clubs: Cancel memberships which you are not using much. Shop around for cheaper deals if you are spending a lot.

These small sacrifices can add up to big savings. As I said before, they will not make a noticeable difference to your immediate quality of life; but they will make a big difference to your future wealth.

There is no doubt that virtually anybody, unless he or she is literally on the breadline, can make savings from previously hidden sources of expenditure. Table 4 has been compiled to help you identify possible reservoirs of potential savings. This list is obviously not exhaustive, there will be other sources of everyday savings that you can think of.

When you are carrying out this exercise, it may be helpful to think of yourself as a small business. You have income and outgoings. In order to make a good profit you need to maximize your income and minimize your outgoings. Every business keeps a tight reign on spending, and periodically this is reviewed by the management.

You too will find it necessary periodically to review your spending, and plan alternatives. It does not take much effort to gain firm control of your finances, and this effort will be amply rewarded. Most people will be pleasantly surprised to find that they can save around ten per cent of their outgoings just by reviewing their budgets and cutting out waste. This amounts to £1,500 a year for the average household! Added to your planned savings this will be more than enough to start you off on your wealth-building programme.

Increasing Your Income

Of course, an equally effective way of looking at the problem of finding the money to invest is to increase your income. You will probably want to do this in tandem with your efforts to cut out wasteful spending. While increasing your income might seem rather a daunting prospect, in fact it is easier than you might suppose.

Your first task when you are seeking to raise your income from its present level is to establish exactly what it is that you most enjoy doing and are best at. Everybody has talents, usually one or two major ones and some minor ones. Expressing these talents is necessary for your happiness and well-being – and if you are able to express them in a business environment, they can be profitable too!

There are countless examples. For instance, if you are good with your hands, think about doing repair work part-time. If you love gardening, then think about how you can exploit the knowledge your hobby has given you by offering your services to other less-skilled gardeners. If you like meeting people and like talking, consider selling a reputable product. Whatever your interest or skill, if you are accomplished you could make money teaching it to others, either on a freelance basis or through more formal outlets, such as in evening classes at a technical college.

If you are not feeling entrepreneurial but still want extra work, then think about working for an organization connected with your hobbies or interests. If you love sailing, you might enjoy being a part-time bar worker at the sailing club!

I stress the importance of doing what you enjoy, because after a full day's work most people feel pretty tired. If they then go out and slave at an additional, part-time job they hate, they are unlikely to keep it up for long, no matter how good the motive. Furthermore, it is a fallacy that the more a job pays the more unpleasant it is. You will only be very successful at jobs that you enjoy, which are those that take your raw talent for the task and channel it in a profitable direction.

Unfortunately, a lot of people think that only particular industries or sectors of the economy are profit-making. In fact you can make a good living at virtually any task, as the number of self-made millionaires doing humble everyday work can testify.

If you are having trouble finding ideas or opportunities, then I would suggest that you put together a 'think-tank' to help you. Enlist the help of at least two willing volunteers, sit yourselves down with a large blank sheet of paper, and write down all the ideas that come to mind, no matter how outlandish they seem at first. It is important at this point that the meeting be conducted without criticism being levelled at anyone's ideas. Once all ideas have been exhausted, they can be further scrutinized, consolidated or whittled down until a solution (or several potential solutions) emerges.

On a more personal level, another method of ideas-generation relates to the practice of meditation, which I would recommend. You will need to find a quiet place to sit and empty your mind, giving no thought to your everyday problems. The more often you do this, the easier it is for your subconscious mind to break through to your conscious one. Your subconscious is the repository of a huge storehouse of ideas and experiences, many of which you find hard to recollect consciously. It is also able to synthesize information from various sources, just as a supercomputer does, and to come up with tailor-made solutions to any problems you may have.

Using the raw material provided by your think-tank plus lots of the other bits of knowledge and memories you have stored away, and assisted by the practice of meditation, your subconscious will begin to offer solutions. You will know that these are workable solutions because they will feel right, and you will feel strongly impelled to put them into practice.

Another benefit of doing what you love to do, especially if it is something that you feel strongly is right for you, is that a momentum will be established that will help carry you along towards success.

With hindsight it may seem uncanny how you managed to be in the right place at the right time, made contact with the right people, and enjoyed breakthroughs which may seem to others to be almost impossible. Once you achieve some small success you will gain enormous confidence, and enter a 'positive feedback loop', where what you do reinforces what you achieved before, propelling you onwards. You may even find that your part-time job eventually becomes your full-time career, provided that it is right for your talents.

Should You Change Your Career?

It is a basic premise of this book that anyone with an income can gain wealth through an effective savings and investment plan, no matter what the circumstances. However, if you feel that your existing income is too low – even with your part-time income and having cut out wasteful spending – then you may want to think seriously about advancing your career or changing your job.

What has been said already about enjoying your work is doubly important for your full-time occupation. After all, it is what you spend half your waking hours doing! Yet too few people seem to find themselves in jobs that they really enjoy.

If you are in this situation, then I would suggest that you begin to plan your way to your next, and enjoyable, appointment. You can do this by deciding first what course you wish to take in your life. In order to get there you are going to need the right qualifications, the right contacts and the necessary experience.

In order to get the right qualifications, I would suggest that you begin right away by going to night school, or by attending training courses on part of your annual leave, instead of taking the usual holiday. You will, of course, enjoy the training, so it will not be any hardship. The money you will need for the course should be considered as a necessary investment in your future prosperity and happiness.

In order to get the right contacts, begin immediately to approach influential decision-makers in the fields in which you wish to excel. Don't be afraid of doing this – people love it when you show genuine interest and enthusiasm for their work, and will go out of their way to help you. This process is called *networking*, and is used extensively in commerce, both formally and informally. For example, professional headhunters use it when they are trying to find people to fill top jobs.

The people you contact may not have an opening for you right away, but they will remember you, especially if you have made face-to-face contact, and will recommend you to others. Remember that 70 per cent of job vacancies are never advertised. Organizations will not necessarily want to go to the expense of advertising if they have the person they require already available.

Lack of experience is not a handicap here, although your attitude might be. If you are going to switch fields entirely, then you will need to begin again, at the bottom. This might actually entail a drop in salary. However, if you are truly convinced that you are in the right field, then you should consider not what you are earning now, but what you will be earning in a few years' time. This will exceed what you would have achieved in your previous field, simply because you are more likely to be successful.

Key Points

- The apparent 'problem' of having insufficient cash can be viewed as an *opportunity* to identify savings and increase your income.

- A periodic review of your spending will reveal many areas in which savings can be made without compromising the quality of your life. These savings can be transferred to your investment programme.

- Part-time work will boost your savings. Try and choose work related to your leisure interests, so it is less like work and more like fun.

- If you hate your job, why not change it? Training opportunities abound, and can be considered as part of your investment programme.

CHAPTER 4

Economic Cycles – and How to Ride Them

Once you have made the decision to save and invest, you are firmly on the way to increasing your wealth. The object of this chapter is to help you pick the right road to maximizing the returns on your investments.

What is discussed in this chapter is based on the simple and natural law of cause and effect. This law is so straightforward that the vast majority of investors have persuaded themselves that it can't be true. They think that natural laws have been repealed by man. This is why so many investors are going to lose money in the 1990s. And why there will be plenty of opportunities for those who understand what is really going on.

The Long Wave

All economic activity is cyclic. Make sure that this fact is engraved on your brain. What goes up must come down. As Scottie would say in *Star Trek*: 'You canna break the laws of physics!'

There are several identifiable cycles. Some are very short, lasting a matter of months. Others last for three to nine years. Business people know that their particular industry will experience cycles of activity, and economists often talk of 'the business cycle', by which they are usually referring to a medium-term cycle affecting the general economy and lasting from four to eight years.

There is however one cycle that is most important of all. It lasts for approximately half a century, and is named after the man who first explained it, Nikolai Kondratieff. It is thus known as the *Kondratieff long wave* (see Figure 1).

Nikolai Kondratieff was an economist living in Russia at the time of the Revolution of 1917. Unfortunately for him what he had to say was not popular with the Communist party, and he ended his days

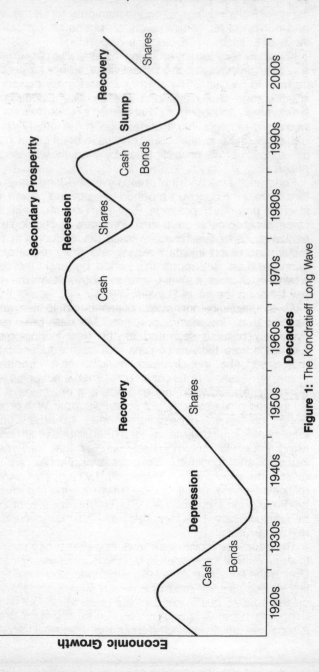

Figure 1: The Kondratieff Long Wave

in one of Stalin's gulags, although thankfully for us this was after he had published his seminal work on economic cycles, 'The Long Wave of Economic Life' (see the Appendix).

Kondratieff noticed, by studying the available data, that there was a regular rhythm to economic activity, spanning a period ranging from 47 to 55 years. This rhythm was far more powerful than the shorter trade cycles that had already been identified by other economists. According to Kondratieff's observation, the world would slide straight into a depression in the late 1920s. And so it did, although Kondratieff could only have been grimly pleased with the success of his prediction, as by then he was languishing in prison.

Kondratieff sketched the anatomy of the long wave as follows. First there is the upwave – a period of sustained growth, picking up from the previous depression. Prices are low, labour is cheap, and, since development costs are low, new technologies can be exploited. Often this recovery takes place during or following a major war, which injects new life into the previously moribund economy. Last time round this period began in the early 1940s, when the UK stock-market began to recover from hitting its all-time low following the fall of Dunkirk in 1940.

As the recovery continues, prices begin to rise and inflation becomes an increasing problem. Markets grow rapidly but eventually become saturated as the new technologies mature. Examples from the recent past include the technologies of the motor car (the industrialized world's most important civilian industry), plastics, antibiotics, consumer electronics, and white goods such as refrigerators and washing machines.

Demand grows steadily, but so does supply. With growth comes rising consumer expectations and industrial unrest. Full employment brings demands for higher wages which coincide with rising prices for commodities such as fuel, raw materials for industry, and foodstuffs. The upwave reaches an inflationary crescendo which is accompanied by mass affluence and a relaxation of the moral codes known during the austere years before the long boom. The end of the upwave of our current generation can be identified as having occurred in the middle-1970s.

The boom then collapses into vicious slump, often ostensibly due to some outside force when in fact the bubble was ripe for bursting. During the early to middle-1970s, the long boom collapsed in the first serious post-war recession, which many people blamed solely on the sudden quadrupling of the price of oil. But its roots were deeper than that. This collapse was unlike any of the previous mild recessions that occurred during the upwave – they were only shallow corrections associated with short-term business cycles. In line with Kondratieff's theories, the recession that marks the end of the upwave is deep, global and long-lasting. It brings with it unemployment previously thought to have been eradicated through sound economic management and careful 'fine tuning' of the economy. The years of the 1950s and 1960s were characterized by full employment, with only 2 to 3 per cent of the work-force jobless at any one time.

When the collapse hit, budding economists like me were taught that unemployment would only be temporary, an aberration that would soon be corrected. The normal level of employment was considered to be full employment. It was believed that the electorate would never tolerate a government which presided over high levels of unemployment.

Kondratieff wrote that after the first recession of the downwave came a plateau period of secondary prosperity. This would last for approximately a decade, after which the world would plunge once again into depression. The famous 'roaring twenties' represented the plateau period preceding the 'Great Depression' of the 1930s.

The plateau period is very interesting in that there is apparent prosperity overlying a growing economic crisis. Financial markets boom and there is an explosion of property prices. People feel richer, and spend a lot. If they don't have the money, they borrow it. Materialism becomes rampant, and Mammon, the god of money, is worshipped as never before. Speculators make a killing in shares and property. More and more people are drawn into speculating in these markets, and popular manias develop.

Does this sound familiar? I'm sure it does – this is a description of the recent past – the 1980s. During this most recent period of secondary prosperity popular speculation concentrated foremost upon property, and also upon shares. Many people mortgaged themselves up to the hilt and bought shares for the first time, especially in the large public corporations becoming newly privatised by the Government.

This prosperity is not sound for the simple reason that underlying markets in the real world are depressed. Agriculture and mining are in the doldrums, with prices falling as deflation takes hold. Real interest rates (the nominal rate minus inflation) rise spectacularly with sharply falling inflation, making people who are in work and earning good salaries feel even richer. Manufacturing recovers somewhat, particularly in the luxury and consumer goods sectors, but there is savage competition. Retailers make good profits on the back of heavy consumer borrowing, but manufacturers have to stay keenly competitive, as the supply of general goods is ample. Unemployment remains high in depressed regions of the nation, hovering at around 10 per cent of the work-force despite the apparent affluence of the remainder of the economy.

The plateau period, which I prefer to call the period of 'false prosperity' tells us that the downwave is already underway. The creation of debt on a massive scale has postponed the days of reckoning, but the price of this debt will mean an even worse depression to come. Eventually the bubble bursts and the whole insubstantial edifice comes crashing down. Many companies and individuals suffer grievously in the process, although others manage to prosper. There are always winners as well as losers at each stage of the long wave.

The 1980s Revisited

I am about to explain why I believe that there will be a global depression in the 1990s. Before doing so I should like to point out that when I talk about a depression it is not because I am by nature a pessimist, or a permanent merchant of doom and gloom. It is just that so many forces are tugging the world economy in the direction of a prolonged downturn that a sober analysis of the facts leads one logically to that conclusion. Forewarned is forearmed. If you know *why* a situation is occurring, then you will be able to protect yourself, and perhaps even profit from the general circumstances.

In fact, a good understanding of the real economy (not the version that we are fed by vested interests) can make you an optimist. Certainly those people who share an understanding of the nature of the long wave will be very bullish just at the point when the majority are convinced that the end of the world is nigh. And that point will soon be here.

I have already briefly explained how the 1980s fit into the general scenario of the long wave. Although according to the theory the secondary prosperity was fully to be expected, and was easily identifiable once underway, the 1980s experience had some special features. These features may well have ensured that the depression facing us in the 1990s will be measurably worse than that experienced by our grandparents in the 1930s.

The first feature is that there were in fact two periods of very nasty recession. The first lasted from 1973 to 1975, the second from 1979 to 1982. Some devotees of Kondratieff's theory believed at the time that the second recession marked the expected plunge into depression following the very short plateau period of the second half of the 1970s. With hindsight, however, we can see that this was merely a respite between what could be seen as one long period of recession.

Another way of looking at this is to say that the 1980s should have experienced a depression but did not. How then was a protracted slump averted? The answer is stark and simple. The USA, the locomotive of the world economy, went on a massive spending spree, turning overseas assets into huge overseas debts.

At the time of the First World War, US Government debt totalled only $1 billion. By 1981 this total had grown to $1,000 billion (£1 trillion). By 1990, the US Government debt had reached a total of $3 trillion and was growing at a rate of more than $5 billion a week! Much of this vast debt was incurred in a huge military build-up, which succeeded in destroying the USSR's ability to compete and hastened the collapse of its economy. Although capitalism has been dancing around the corpse of communism in recent times, there remains the problem of debt in the capitalist world, which is likely to make the USA's (and hence the world's) subsequent depression that much worse.

During the 1970s, the governments of the industrializing Third World countries such as Mexico, Brazil, Argentina, Nigeria, Indonesia and the like borrowed hugely against the spiralling prices of oil and other commodities. By the 1980s deflation had arrived and defaults on the debts had threatened the very core of the world banking system. New sources of debt-creation were required to keep the false boom going. When the US Government kick-started its economy out of the slump of the early 1980s with its borrowing splurge much of the rest of the developed world followed suit. Now it was the turn of Western companies and Western consumers to clamour for credit. The banks were happy to oblige as their profits boomed.

By the time of the great stock-market crash of 1987 the world had become a debt junkie, thoroughly hooked on credit. We have already noted that US Government debt totalled some $3 trillion. To that we can add another $1 trillion of Third World debt, plus an extra $4 to $5 trillion for corporate and consumer debts. There is actually so much debt in issue that it is difficult to estimate its full extent! Perhaps the best measure to use is that employed by D. and W. Kirkland in their book *Power Cycles* (see the Appendix). They estimate that just before the depression of the 1930s the ratio of debt to currency in circulation plus gold reached 15:1. During the depths of the slump the ratio contracted to 5:1 as debt was repudiated. The ratio today is nearer 30:1.

Another salient point which seems to have escaped the attention of many people is the scope of the financial crash of 1987. During the famous Wall Street crash of 1929 the immediate fall in the markets was of the order of 12 per cent from its 1929 peak. Later the markets were to fall by more than 80 per cent. During the 1987 crash, the immediate fall in London and New York was around 22 per cent in two days – almost twice as bad as that of 1929.

Since then, of course bankers and politicians have been assuring us that the crash was an aberration, engendered by computer trading. The stock-market's subsequent recovery to new heights seemed to confirm this interpretation. So just in case you are also feeling complacent, it is worth dipping into a theory of market behaviour which has proved remarkably accurate.

Elliot Wave Theory

Ralph Elliot was an accountant who made an exhaustive study of the American stock-market. He believed that there was a regular pattern of stock-market behaviour which could be traced and which would allow the astute investor to make good profits. The basic pattern described by Elliot took the form of five waves – three up and two down (labelled waves 1–5 in Figure 2). This would then be followed by a three-wave formation, taking the form of two down and one up (labelled A, B, and C in Figure 2). These complementary wave formations would repeat endlessly, and could therefore be studied on a daily, monthly, yearly or 10-yearly basis. Each set of waves would be called a cycle.

Figure 2 illustrates a simplified version of a very long cycle lasting from 1932 to the present and showing the peaks and troughs of market activity. You can see that the bear phase, which began in October 1987, has yet to be completed. A general pattern is indicated, although of course there is no guarantee that the reality will conform to the theory.

There is no doubt that these waves can be discerned, but sometimes they are very obscure. This doesn't really matter if you are investing for the long-term and can ignore temporary fluctuations, as long as you pick the right trend. Elliot's followers got very excited around 1982, when they confidently predicted a glorious bull market which would take the stock-market indices to previously unheard-of heights. People like the American Robert Prechter made millions of dollars predicting and profiting from this wave, as did other people who followed his lead. Of course, the Elliot-wave disciples were in general correct. The more it seemed that their forecasts were accurate, the more they were heeded. However, the message of what would happen after the great bull run of the 1980s has not been widely disseminated. You have to do a bit of research to find out what the theory says will come next.

The Elliot wave theory and its current gurus predict a very different future for the stock-market for the rest of the century. According to their interpretation a major corrective wave is now under way. This takes the form of an extra large correction marking

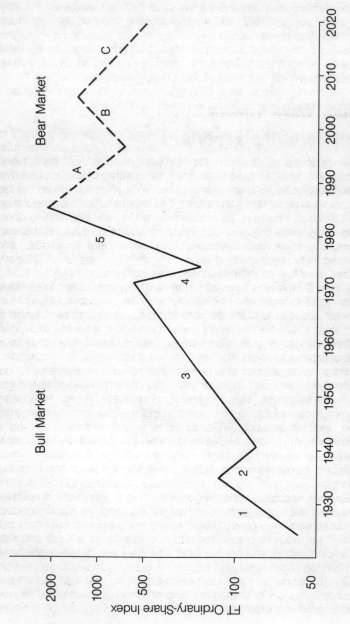

Figure 2: The Simplified Elliot Wave as Applied to the UK Stock-market

the end of the supercycle of stock-market activity that began in 1932. According to the theory, we have had five waves on the way up, culminating in 1987, and we should have three on the way down (two down and one up).

You will note immediately that the supercycle described by Elliot sounds very similar to the Kondratieff long wave. In fact, the only overall difference seems that the stock-market tends to act as an early-warning device, so it crashes ahead of the depression and begins its recovery during the slump itself.

Beware of the Experts

This description of two very important theories has been necessarily brief. I would urge you to read some of the books listed in the Appendix to learn more. I shall restrain myself from saying more, because others such as Robert Beckman, Christopher Wood and Robert Prechter have already done an excellent job of explaining these theories. For the purposes of your future financial well-being, however, I will make some points here for you to bear in mind in future.

First, very few economists, politicians, bankers, estate agents and the like believe in theories. This is partly because they have persuaded themselves that economies can be managed. In truth it is very difficult to manage something that is driven by billions of decisions made every day by people who do not for the most part behave rationally but rather emotionally. Social psychology is a better subject to study than economics if you really want to understand why the economy is subject to booms and slumps.

On the other hand, people who do believe the theories tend to be highly successful businessmen and investors. Those in the know do not, however, generally shout about it. They just quietly profit from their knowledge. This explains why investors like James Goldsmith and Lord Hanson foresaw the chaos in the stock-markets and moved into cash. They have also been careful to invest in basic industries which will survive slumps and profit during booms.

Second, vested interests will tell you what it is in *their* interests for you to believe. Estate agents will tell you that another housing boom is just around the corner. Stockbrokers will tell you that shares are always the best long-term investment. Politicians will tell you that recessions either will not happen, or if they are clearly underway, will only be short-lived. And bankers will tell you that you can always afford to borrow lots of money – unless of course their banks are already in trouble from previous excess lending, in which case they can turn off the credit tap abruptly!

It takes a lot of courage to make your own analysis and go your own way. Yet if you want to make the most of your hard-earned savings this is what you must do. The most successful investors are those who are able to pick the correct economic trend and invest with it. If you have done this you don't need to worry about short-term market fluctuations. We shall consider appropriate investment strategies in the next chapter, following a further excursion into the psychology of investing.

The Economic Outlook

The value of the Kondratieff long wave is not only that it explains very cogently *why* we are in the economic situation in which we find ourselves at any given time, but also *what we can expect for the immediate future.* I know of no other explanation of how the world works which will allow us to do this. The information can be uncannily accurate, so much so that some analysts reject it out of hand, saying history cannot repeat itself so exactly.

The extraordinary fact is that here and now history *is* repeating itself. The parallels between the experiences of the 1920s and 1930s and their near-equivalents in the 1980s and 1990s are quite awesome. Yet economists and politicians cannot bring themselves to believe that the boom-and-bust cycle is a part of mass human psychology. This is because they fervently wish, or need to believe, that they can control the manifold decisions of consumers and producers by wielding the blunt instruments of interest rates and patterns of Government spending. If this really were the case, unemployment rates would be stable, as would interest rates, the money supply, and all the other indicators so closely watched by decision-makers.

Just to let you know how much faith one can have in the Kondratieff theory, allied to Elliot wave theory, I am willing to write down some predictions which will help you to invest in the years to come. Many of these predictions are already coming true but were considered by mass opinion to be unthinkable or impossible only a few years ago.

1. Trade war is becoming a real danger. Trade barriers will increase and the major trading blocs of the USA/Canada and the EEC will seek to keep out imports from countries outside their sphere of influence.
2. Unemployment will continue to rise as the current recession deepens and becomes a depression. Taxes on the earnings of those who remain employed will rise, as the burden of welfare expenditure grows.

3. <u>Social unrest</u> will grow and crimes against property will continue to increase.
4. <u>Residential property values will continue to fall for at least a decade. Any upturns will be short-lived.</u>
5. Agricultural land will also continue to fall in value over the same period, as more and more <u>farmers go bankrupt.</u>
6. Oil and other <u>commodity prices will fall</u> over the long term, unless artificially supported within trading blocs or temporarily increased by war.
7. Western aid to Third World countries will decrease. Indebted countries will default wholesale on their obligations to Western banks and governments. <u>Major Western banks will either go bankrupt or have to be rescued by their governments.</u>
8. <u>Assuming Elliot wave theory is correct, stock-markets should fall to around two-thirds of their peak values, rally, and then fall again even further to levels not seen since the 1960s and</u> 1970s.
9. Social values will change radically. Conspicuous consumption will be out, and <u>neighbourly behaviour</u> will be in. People will borrow less and <u>save more.</u>
10. The slump will give way to a <u>sustained recovery, probably in the early part of the twenty-first century.</u>

I could go on at some length. Those authors already mentioned above have done so, and you might like to consult the Appendix for a list of appropriate texts. All of these authors well understand the long wave yet have faced ridicule for their prognostications. None the less, they are already being proved correct.

A stiff dose of realism is always necessary for successful investors. You must consider things as they are – not as you might wish them to be! <u>Most of the commentary you read in newspapers and magazines is of the opposite variety – it is full of optimistic nonsense based on what the authors feel is acceptable to themselves and their readers. So-called expert opinions on house prices come foremost in this category.</u>

Having said this, I must repeat that <u>I am still an optimist!</u> There is no reason to abandon a savings and investment programme in the midst of a slump – indeed, there is all the more reason to accumulate cash so that assets can be purchased at a fraction of their former values. A good understanding of the real state of the economy and its likely direction will allow you to profit from the long wave. That way you can maintain your ambitions and forge ahead in what others perceive to be difficult times.

The Way Ahead

Since I began to write about what I have long believed and understood, the economy has unfolded much as I anticipated. Even the Gulf war – an apparent wild card – had its roots substantially in the debt of Iraq and its need to push up the price of oil, which had been subject to strong deflationary pressures. The economic slump has intensified, with firms large and small going under, unemployment rising sharply, and inflation falling.

As you read this we are quite probably in the depths of global depression. Or, to put it another way, the global depression which already exists will have eaten its way even into prosperous areas and will be recognized publicly as a problem. This is precisely the point where pessimists (i.e., realists) become optimists. Already there are bargains to be had among certain shares – bargains that you may never see again. The same will eventually be true of property. Bonds and cash are still offering good returns.

In short, this is a saver's and investor's paradise! What a wonderful time to begin your investment programme! But many people around you are in shock at the extent of the downturn, so the emotional climate may be negative and anti-investment. It is as hard for the average investor to buy at the bottom as it is to sell at the top. This is why it is important that you read the next chapter carefully, to understand how profitable it can be to become a *contrarian* – someone who generally does the opposite of what the majority of investors are doing.

Kondratieff theory tells us that after the slump comes the long boom. Imagine how rich your family would be today if your parents could have bought shares at 1940s prices and held on to them until the 1970s! You can take advantage of experience, and make fantastic gains.

Key Points

- All economic activity is cyclic. There are cycles of different duration and cycles that affect different industries. All economists agree on this fact.

- The most powerful cycle of all is the Kondratieff long wave, lasting about half a century. Many economists do not like to accept this theory, despite considerable evidence supporting it, as it negates their self-appointed role as 'fine tuners' of the economy.

- Mass human sentiment drives market economies, which depend on billions of decisions made daily by their participants. They are not therefore easily subject to government control.

- The slump is here, but it is nothing to be afraid of. This is a wonderful time to begin an investment programme!

CHAPTER 5

Risks and Rewards

Investment is always a trade-off between risk and reward. All types of investment lie along a spectrum which goes from the ultra-safe to ultra-risky. Your investment position will be subject to three main considerations. The first is your financial circumstances and the second your character. Some people are naturally cautious, while others like to gamble.

The third major factor which will influence your investment programme is the stage the economy has reached along the Kondratieff long wave. At each stage of the cycle crucial indicators point to the set of investments which are appropriate to the circumstances. From these you can deduce what mixture of investments are likely to be successful, and then decide on the degree of risk you wish to take with each.

It is not difficult to invest effectively, as long as you are able to turn a deaf ear to the voice of mass opinion which will try to sway you, often pointing you in the wrong direction completely! Mass opinion, much of which is shaped by vested interests, is what you read most of the time in newspapers and magazines, hear daily on the radio or see on TV. It is therefore very pervasive, and difficult to ignore. In the short term the herd can be right, but in the long term it is invariably wrong.

In this chapter I shall discuss the primary investment features that will be of importance to you. The first is *the psychology of investment*, that is, those characteristics necessary if you are to become a successful investor. The second is *investment indicators* – you must learn to study these in order to gain a proper understanding of the pace and direction of the economy. The third is *basic types of investment* – the three main investment vehicles (cash, bonds and shares) and how they fit into the long wave and can maximize your returns at different stages of the economic cycle.

The Psychology of Investment

The fundamental point about effective investment is the search for value. Obviously you will want to buy assets when they are cheap, and sell them when they are expensive. In other words, the successful investor should always be on the lookout for assets that are *undervalued*.

While this observation may appear to be obvious, a cursory investigation into the behaviour of most investors reveals that they do the exact opposite. They pile into fashionable areas of investment when these areas are close to maturity, and bail out while their values are falling or when prices have hit rock bottom.

A classic example of this was evident in the middle-1980s. The stock-market had shot up from 1982, and some investors and traders were making fortunes. This gradually came to the attention of the media, and thence the general public. A share boom developed, with millions of people partaking in share investment for the first time, either directly or through unit trusts.

When the bubble burst in October 1987 there was widespread panic. Many of the new investors were unaware that the market could fall so heavily in such a short time – down nearly a third in less than a month. They sold out in droves. The unit trusts, which had been receiving record inflows of funds of the order of £1 billion in 1987, experienced a net outflow of £200 million the following year. Yet many of the investors who cashed their shares in a panic would have done well to have waited for the inevitable rally which followed the crash. By 1989 the market had reached new record heights.

Here we must absorb one of the most useful investment maxims, coined by Baron Rothschild: 'Always leave a profit for the other fellow.' It is precisely when the market is reaching its most euphoric peak that you must sell out and move into another investment arena. Yet most people choose this moment at which to rush in and buy.

It is equally the case that the investor must summon up the courage to buy when the situation looks most bleak. The British stock-market reached its all-time low in 1940, with the fall of Dunkirk. At this point the index touched 49.4. However, 28 years later it reached 520, a more than ten-fold gain. A person with courage, foresight and spare cash could have cleaned up by purchasing undervalued shares in 1940, when it looked as if Britain was about to fail in its war against the Axis powers.

It may not surprise you to hear that this illustrates another Rothschild maxim: 'The time to buy is when blood is running on the streets.' This very famous investment principle is based on Rothschild's most staggering coup. In 1812, Wellington's army was about to confront Napoleon's at Waterloo. The prize was European economic domination. If England lost it would have had a devastating effect on her manufactures and trade.

Rothschild had invested heavily in a network of informers, and received news of Wellington's victory before his rivals did. Instead of buying stocks, however, he sold them. This created a panic on the London stock-exchange, as other investors reasoned that the battle must have been lost. As the mob sold and shares reached rock bottom, Rothschild stepped in and bought again. Hours later, news of the victory reached London and the market took off. Rothschild made an estimated £1 million from this ploy – a staggering fortune in the early 19th century.

You are probably consumed with admiration for Rothschild's courage and guile. Most people would have bought rather than sold at the news. Given that we are not all of Rothschild's temperament, we can at least learn the lesson of courageous investing at market troughs.

A word of warning is necessary here. If the market is going down in a long bear move (when prices fall), you should be careful to ensure that the bottom really is the bottom, and not one of a series of downward steps. During the crash of 1929 – 32, many investors lost their shirts through premature investment, only to see the index reach new lows, wiping out the value of their share portfolios.

When a market is crashing after a long period of exceptional increases, the majority of people believe that the latest fall will be only short-lived, and that things will soon return to normal. The time horizon of many investors is very short, their collective memories do not go back very far, and few have bothered to study economic history. For the majority, the crash of 1987 has been largely disregarded; the bear market of 1972–74 is but a vague memory; and the experience of the 1930s is considered ancient history, irrelevant to modern times.

The Kondratieff wave and the Elliot wave theory tell us that the early 1990s are remarkably rare and exciting times, when the stock-market is headed a long way down. This represents a crisis for some and an opportunity for others. Assuming that the patterns of the past offer realistic clues for the future, astute investors are even now accumulating cash to take part in one of the most profitable investment moves of their lifetime. They are readying themselves to buy undervalued quality shares when the economic news is bleakest.

Yet as the market falls some will invest too soon, believing the incessant comment in the press that 'shares are looking cheap at these prices'. As their portfolios continue to fall, many will greet the first upward rally off the true bottom as an opportunity to sell out.

It is precisely at this point that the investor should be buying. Investment is thus both an art and a science. Some people really do have a genuine 'feel' for it. But there are indicators which can help the rest of us to decide when a market has reached its peak or trough.

Investment Indicators

Probably the best way to value any investment is to consider the ratios relevant to it, and the range over which these ratios travel during the life of the long wave. We can use an example with which many people are familiar – house prices.

There are two key ratios that one can use when attempting to assess the 'value' of houses. By this I mean their financial value. There is of course another form of value, known to economists as 'utility value'. Utility value is a description of the benefit you get from using something. Shares have no utility value (you can't do anything useful with them), but houses have.

We can assess the financial value of a house either in terms of its affordability or in terms of its value as an investment. If you are interested in living in a house primarily for its utility value, then the first question you will be asking is whether or not it is affordable. This in turn will depend upon your household income and its relationship to the price of the house. Over the last generation or so, average house price-to-income ratios have varied, but have generally been in the range of 2 to 3 times average incomes. Sometimes however the ratio has moved outside that range, such as during the housing boom of 1985–88, when it reached as high as 5 times average incomes.

For observers of this key ratio of housing affordability, the price slump of 1988–90 was no surprise. Prices had to fall back into line with potential home-owners' ability to pay. Yet at the time many home-buyers were caught up in an emotional frenzy, believing that if they did not jump on the bandwagon immediately they would never be able to get on at all.

There is another way of looking at house prices, which is to consider the ratio of the rent a house can get as compared to its price. At present this ratio, expressed as a percentage of the house value, ranges from around 4 per cent to 8 per cent. You might then ask yourself, if you are considering the purchase of a house for its investment rather than utility value, whether it is a good investment.

Suppose that you could get an 8 per cent rental return on the house, but that if you left the price of the house in cash in the bank you could get 12 per cent after taxes. Your 8 per cent return on the house would have to include management and maintenance charges on the property, and would also be taxed. This might reduce the return to, say, 5 per cent. Unless you were very confident of a substantial increase in the price of the house, you would be unlikely to go ahead and purchase it on investment grounds alone.

The existence of a rental market would also influence a decision made on utilitarian grounds. In economists' jargon you would want to maximize utility at minimal cost. If interest rates were very high, and you were paying, for example, 14 per cent per annum mortgage interest, then you might find it more economical to rent a house. In this case you would find it much cheaper to rent property than to 'rent' money, that is, have a mortgage. I myself am currently renting a house at one-third of the rate it would cost me to buy it.

The same type of ratio analysis would be relevant if you bought the house entirely with cash. If it cost £100,000 to buy, and bank interest rates were 12 per cent, then the cost of not putting the money in the bank would be £12,000 a year. Economists call this 'opportunity cost' – the opportunity foregone by doing one thing rather than another. If on the other hand you could rent the same house for £6,000 a year, because properties were currently yielding 6 per cent, then you might prefer to keep the money in the bank, using half of the interest as rent and investing the remainder.

Of course, all of these decisions would have to include a reasonable assessment of the outlook for interest rates. Much of our investment analysis will depend upon this key ratio – the rent that money can make as a reward for the opportunity cost of one person lending it to another.

Popular opinion firmly asserts that houses are the best long-term

Table 5: Key Ratios: Buying vs Renting a House

House market value		=	£100,000	
Buying:				
Deposit		=	£ 20,000	
Opportunity cost of deposit @ 12%		=	£ 2,400	p.a.
Cost of £80,000 mortgage @ 12%		=	£ 9,431	p.a.
Maintenance and building insurance @ 0.5%	=	£ 500	p.a.
Total		=	**£ 12,331**	**p.a.**
Renting:				
Annual rent at 8%		=	£ 8,000	p.a.
Saving		=	£ 4,331	p.a.
Annual rent at 6%		=	£ 6,000	p.a.
Saving		=	£ 6,331	p.a.

investment. You can see from Table 5 that this is not always the case – it depends upon where in the long wave economic cycle we are, and upon the key ratios relevant to house prices. You do not have to have an advanced degree in mathematics to calculate these ratios. You only need to know what to look for.

In the following chapters we shall consider what ratios and measures of value are of importance for each type of investment. We may conclude here with a brief description of the three main types of investment vehicles (cash, bonds and shares) and their role in your investment strategy for each stage of the long wave.

Basic Types of Investment
Cash

The first type of investment you can consider is simply keeping your money in cash. A lot of people do not consider this to be a proper investment, but it can be very appropriate. When times are uncertain and the stock-market is falling, cash can outperform every other type of investment. For example, money market (cash) funds were top of the league among unit trusts performance in 1990, during the bear market for shares.

Today, investment in cash doesn't have to be boring. There are a variety of ways of investing cash in bank and building society accounts, with National Savings, or through money market-funds. Some of the available accounts pay interest tax-free at very attractive rates. Given the power of compound interest already discussed in chapter 2, plus the current high levels of real interest rates (after inflation), you should give cash investment your serious consideration. We shall discuss the merits of the various schemes in chapter 6.

Cash is good for uncertain times, when other markets have become overvalued and are likely to fall. It is doubly attractive when real interest rates are high. You can see from the diagram of the idealized long wave (Figure 1, page 33) that cash is most attractive towards the end of the era of false prosperity, when real interest rates (allowing for inflation) are at their highest for the entire long wave cycle. This contrasts with times of high inflation, such as was experienced during the early 1970s, when real interest rates can be negative – which means that they are lower than inflation. Even if interest rates are nominally high, at, say, 17 per cent, you are still losing money in real terms if inflation is at 20 per cent or more, which was the case in the late 1970s.

Bonds

Bonds are the next important category of investment. A bond is

simply a promise to pay a fixed interest rate on a nominal sum
of money. For example, a bond may have a face value of £100,
and will pay 10 per cent interest every year. So you make £10 a
year. This is guaranteed by the company or government that issues
the bond. Bonds are famous for doing well during times of low
inflation, when real interest rates are high. They also do well when
interest rates are falling.

The reason why it is good to hold bonds when interest rates are
falling is that their money value rises to reflect the new level of
interest rates. If a bond pays 10 per cent and interest rates are
cut to 8 per cent, it will rise in value to reflect this new state of
affairs. Now the bond will be worth £125 (8 per cent of £125 =
£10). The bond always pays £10 a year interest on its face value
of £100. Conversely, if interest rates rise, the market value of the
bond will fall. In this example a 2.5 per cent rise in interest rates
from 10 to 12.5 per cent will cause the bond to fall in value to £80,
as £10 = 12.5 per cent of £80.

Bonds are issued by governments, other public bodies such as
local authorities, and companies. Governments of rich countries
such as the USA and the UK are unlikely to default, and so their
bonds are considered very safe. Because they are low-risk, their
interest rates are relatively low. The greater the risk of default, the
greater the yield of the bond. Governments of Latin American
countries such as Argentina and Brazil which run a high risk of
defaulting issued bonds a decade or so ago which are now trading
at only a fraction of their face value.

Because US Treasury bonds and UK Treasury bonds (the latter
are known as *gilts*) are very low-risk, they are favoured by investors
when there are doubts about the stability of the world economy.
For example, should there be the threat of a generalized banking
crisis in the USA, investors will fly to put their money in bonds, not
only because they pay a relatively stable yield but also because
their value is ultimately guaranteed by the US Government. This
is not always true of cash. In the UK depositors only enjoy limited
protection for the first £20,000 of their cash invested – 75 per cent
protection for bank accounts and 90 per cent for building society
accounts.

Because bonds do so well in times of uncertainty and when
interest rates are falling, they are favoured by investors when the
Kondratieff long wave is moving towards the bottom of its range,
during the depression period. They are also useful as a short-term
investment during smaller recessions. Bond investment is
discussed more fully in chapter 9.

Shares

Shares come into their own when the economy begins its long haul back to prosperity. The period from 1940 through to the early 1970s saw spectacular gains for shares (or equities, as they are otherwise known). Shares also perform well during the period of secondary prosperity, as we saw during the 1980s.

Many financial advisers will tell you that you should always invest in shares if you want to go for capital growth. Unfortunately, this is not always the case. Just because the last 30 years have been good for share investment does not automatically mean that the next 30 will repeat the process. The pattern of the long wave tells us that we are now at the end of the overall cycle, in the dangerous final bear market. Only when this has ended will it be safe to invest in shares again. However, those who do so when the nadir of the crisis is reached and there is almost universal gloom will prosper mightily in the next upwave. Those who do not could see their paper wealth evaporate and will have a long time to wait before they recover their losses.

Many investment advisers and pension fund managers also believe that investment portfolios should be highly diversified in order to spread risk. Again, this misreads the conditions of the real economy. Investors would do better to hold most of their assets in only one or two of the three general classes of investment at any particular stage of the economic cycle. This way maximum performance can be wrung from each. Shares will not always do well when bonds are booming, for example. The long wave shows us that towards the end of the downwave investment in shares should be avoided in favour of cash and bonds.

Other potential forms of investment such as precious metals, land and property tend to do well when inflation is booming, towards the end of the upwave. They do far less well when inflation and the stock-market are falling, at which point they can lose ground rapidly in real terms. However, gold has a special role to play during the depression period if currencies return to the gold standard, as we shall see in chapter 11.

Key Points

- Investors can make good steady gains, and avoid the wilder fluctuations of the stock-market by understanding basic social psychology. Value is only found where the majority is *not* looking.

- Always pay attention to key ratios which give robust indications of the real value of each category of investment.

- The role of interest rates is crucial. When they are high, cash is attractive. When falling, bonds boom. When low, shares are likely to do well.

- Assess the general investment climate within the context of the long wave so that you can follow the appropriate investment strategies, ones that suit the particular circumstances of the times.

CHAPTER 6

Cash Can Be King

Before embarking on more sophisticated forms of investment you will want to ensure that you are managing your everyday cashflow well, and that you have sufficient reserves of ready money to meet any sudden demands. You may also want to consider some of the attractive rewards simply of investing part of your spare money in cash. We will start with the basics – your current account.

Current Accounts

Up until a few years ago the majority of high street banks did not pay interest on current accounts. This meant that they could take deposits from their customers every day and reinvest them on short-term money markets, adding hugely to their own profits. Competitive pressures gradually emerged, however – spearheaded by the introduction of building society current accounts in the 1980s – and forced the banks to begin paying interest on their cheque accounts.

Despite this breakthrough not all existing customers have actually switched to interest-bearing current accounts. If you are in this category, it would be good idea do so. It is also worth shopping around for the best deal, as rates can vary quite a lot. Table 6 shows a sample of the current rates offered by the larger banks and building societies.

You can see that there is as much as a threefold difference in rates of interest paid on current accounts. On a monthly average balance of £1,000, this could add up to £40 per year! Remember, all the extra interest you earn can be put towards your investment programme.

Another important feature of most bank current accounts, again introduced only relatively recently, is that as long as you remain in credit you do not have to pay bank charges. These would otherwise be quite heavy, varying from £0.50–£1.00 per debit, as well as a

Table 6: Annual Interest Credited to Cheque Accounts (£1,000 balance, 1991 figures)

Barclays	3.5
National Westminster	2.0
Midland	3.75
Firstdirect (Midland)	6.0
Lloyds	3.0
Bank of Scotland	4.25
Abbey National	4.0
Halifax	6.0

possible standing charge. If you do not have a prior arrangement with your bank, you may also be forced to pay a punitive rate of interest on any overdraft. So it is vital that you at least plan to break even each month. Having cash on deposit to meet unexpected expenditures will help you to achieve this goal.

Deposit Accounts

Most banks and building societies that offer current accounts for your everyday banking requirements will also provide deposit accounts which offer a higher rate of interest. While the rates offered are nowhere near as attractive as those which are possible elsewhere, short-term cash balances and emergency money should be parked where it is easily accessible as well as earning the best rate you can get. Again, you should shop around for the best deals.

Another type of account worth considering for emergency money or for larger purchases is a cheque account which pays a high rate of interest in exchange for your keeping a high minimum balance. This can range from as little as £500 to as much as £2,500. Most accounts of this type also offer tiered interest rates, which rise as your account balance increases beyond each interest-rate threshold.

Credit Cards

If you are disciplined, credit cards can be excellent tools for cash management, enabling you to enjoy free credit while earning interest on the money in your current account which would otherwise have been spent on the goods and services you have bought using the credit card. You can also enjoy a degree of protection from faulty goods or from possible insolvency of the company selling the goods or services. For example, if you buy an item of furniture and pay by credit card, and then while you are awaiting delivery the firm goes bust, you should have little difficulty reclaiming the money from your credit card company, which will in turn sue the retailer. It would be difficult to reclaim the money if you had paid cash.

But if you find that you do not have sufficient money in your account to repay the debt at the end of the credit period (usually four to six weeks from the date of purchase), then you will stand to lose heavily. Credit card interest rates are exceptionally high. Currently, they range from 20 to 35 per cent a year, depending upon the type of card used. If you find that you persistently overspend on credit cards, then you would be better off destroying the ones you have. However, if you can use credit cards in a controlled manner in lieu of cash purchases, then by all means do so and enjoy the benefits and convenience.

One reliable way of ensuring that the balance is paid off in full is to arrange for your bank to deduct the necessary amount from your current account and pay it to the credit card account on a regular direct debit basis. This will ensure that you pay no interest charges at all. You should also avoid paying an annual registration fee to the credit card company. Many banks now insist on this but some do not, and it may be worth switching your credit card account to one that does not include a yearly charge.

Credit Management Strategies

If you want to get wealthy you will avoid unnecessary borrowing. The only reason you might need to borrow money for personal finance purposes is to buy a home, where you are saving rent; or to buy a car or other large semi-essential item which you can't afford to purchase outright.

At the current stage of the long economic cycle, interest rates are exceptionally high in real terms. This makes borrowing very expensive, as people who have taken on large mortgages have already discovered. Therefore, even if you have borrowed money for a large purchase such as a house or car, you may wish to find ways of paying off the loan early. We shall discuss how you may do this with your mortgage in chapter 7.

For other personal loans, where you may be considering borrowing the money from a bank, building society or finance company, it is wise to shop around for the best deal. There is always some variation between financial institutions in the amount of interest charged on personal loans. With even the lowest interest rates, current rates of 20 per cent or more ensure that you will repay almost two-thirds more than the amount borrowed over the period of the loan if it is five years or longer (remember the power of compound interest). However, the final interest charge will be much lower if you can arrange to repay the loan quickly. So apart from shopping around for the best deal, you may also want to ensure that you take out a loan over a relatively short period of, say, one to three years.

In general, personal loans are not to be recommended. You are nearly always better off going without until you can save up a cash sum and negotiate a hefty discount on the required item. However, credit terms are acceptable where the price is reasonable and *interest-free* credit is offered. This is becoming increasingly common among retailers fighting for business, whereas once it was rare on the high street. You may even get interest-free credit for periods of a year or more on the price of a car. Even if you have the cash to buy an item outright, it may still be worth taking on interest-free credit so that your cash can earn interest over the period of the loan.

Periods of prolonged recession are wonderful for cash buyers, who can negotiate excellent discounts on sale prices or take advantage of widespread interest-free credit combined with discount prices. Enjoy it while it lasts, and make as much extra interest as possible on your cash balances at the bank. Cream off the interest paid each month for your investment programme.

Longer-term Cash Savings

Having taken action to ensure that a) you are squeezing the maximum possible benefit from your everyday cash management; b) you have eliminated unnecessary debt, and c) you have accumulated sufficient funds to pay for emergencies; you may wish to consider some longer-term savings schemes which offer high interest rates and absolute safety for your funds. These will be at the core of your investment programme, allowing you to be more adventurous with other surplus savings.

TESSA Accounts

TESSA stands for Tax Exempt Special Savings Account. Introduced by the British Government in January 1991, this type of account allows you to save a maximum of £9,000 in a special fund which grows free of tax over a minimum period of five years. You are allowed to invest an initial £3,000 in the first year, and a maximum of £1,800 annually thereafter, up to the £9,000 limit. This represents quite a bonus, especially for people who have to pay a higher rate of taxes.

To take an example, if you are a higher-rate taxpayer and you open a TESSA account at 12 per cent interest, your money will double in only six years. If you had to pay tax at 40 per cent, as with a conventional savings account, your money would take 10 years to double, as the interest rate would effectively be reduced to 7.2 per cent. For ordinary-rate taxpayers, the interest rate of a conventional savings account would be reduced to only 9 per cent, meaning that it would take 8 years for the money you had deposited to double in size.

Interest rates do, of course, vary over time. Yet there are ways of ensuring that you get a guaranteed rate of return on your cash over a five-year period. This can be done through various schemes offered by National Savings.

National Savings Schemes

National Savings are a Government institution with which we are all very familiar. As children we are likely to have opened a National Savings account at our local post office. Curiously, later in life many investors overlook the schemes offered by National Savings in favour of the apparently more exciting returns possible in the stock-market or other investment arenas.

It is a mistake to dismiss National Savings schemes as boring and outdated. After all, they offer guaranteed returns which are absolutely safe. Sometimes these returns can be very attractive, with high real rates of interest or tax concessions. Also, National Savings is a Government institution, which will never go bust, whereas your bank or building society could do so.

National Savings offer a variety of products. Information and application forms are available from Post Offices. Apart from ordinary current accounts and deposit accounts, the merits of which can be assessed alongside comparable bank and building society accounts, there are several other attractive schemes, which are discussed in detail below.

The Yearly Plan

This is a good way to get your savings plan started. You elect to save a monthly sum by standing order for 12 months. At the end of this period you are issued with a certificate which you hold for a further four years. Your savings will earn a fixed interest rate, free of tax. Although the interest rate may be below prevailing bank and building society rates, if you believe that interest rates will fall in the future, you may like to consider locking into what is likely to become an attractive rate.

The yearly plan is also a good way to get into the savings habit. The money will be deducted automatically from your bank account.

Although you can cash in your certificates before the full qualifying period has elapsed, you will not be encouraged to do so because the rate of interest paid will be lower.

The interest paid on the plan fluctuates from year to year, although it is fixed once you have entered into any specific agreement. The amounts you may save monthly vary from £20 to £200.

Savings Certificates

These offer terms similar to those of the yearly plan. You buy the certificates in units of £25, and keep them for five years. Again, they will earn interest free of tax. The rates payable are usually the same as those offered to savers in the yearly plan.

Savers are allowed to hold up to £5,000 in savings certificates. Reinvestment is encouraged from both mature yearly plans and mature savings certificate issues, up to a maximum of £10,000 on top of the normal limit. You may cash in all or part of the certificates at any time, but it is wise to keep them until the end of the term in order to earn maximum interest.

Income Bonds

These are similar to savings certificates, except that they pay interest on a monthly basis. Interest is paid gross, making the bonds attractive to non-taxpayers. Interest rates are competitive. The minimum that can be invested is £2,000, with a maximum of £25,000.

Income bonds are also issued by a variety of banks, building societies and insurance companies. The terms and conditions vary, and it is best to consult a financial broker or the pages of a professional financial journal to find the bond which best suits your circumstances. Most pay interest gross, so if you are a taxpayer it will have to be declared on your annual return.

Index-Linked Certificates

These are issued at intervals – the fifth issue is currently in circulation. The fifth issue offers an attractive real rate of interest. If you hold your certificates for the full five years, you will receive interest calculated as inflation (as measured by the retail price index) plus 4.5 per cent. Your dividends are not subject to income tax. This compares with real interest rates on an ordinary building society account of nearer 2 per cent. With inflation at an average of 6 per cent, your money will double in a little under 7 years.

You are allowed to save a minimum of £25 and a maximum of £10,000 in index-linked certificates. Should you want to reinvest your profits in the next issue, the limits may be increased, subject to rules current at the time.

Capital Bonds

These are suitable for non-taxpayers who wish to earn interest gross at a guaranteed rate over a set period. The bonds are bought and held for five years, over which period they guarantee to return the interest rate which applied at the time they were purchased, regardless of what has happened to interest rates in the meantime. So if you expect interest rates to fall substantially, you might want to consider this form of cash saving.

The minimum purchase is £100, with further purchases in multiples of £100. As with other National Savings products, you can cash in all or part of the bond at any time, but you will receive a reduced interest rate, or no interest at all if the bonds are cashed within the first year of purchase. Neither do capital bonds pay interest after the five-year holding period is up – they must be cashed at maturity.

Foreign Currency Accounts

Apart from taking advantage of the safety of National Savings, or the competitiveness of it and other forms of cash savings with banks and building societies, you may wish to keep some of your cash in foreign currencies. If you open accounts denominated in the Deutschmark, Swiss franc or the US dollar, you can benefit from favourable movements in that currency relative to the pound. If, for example, a US-dollar account pays 8 per cent interest a year and the pound depreciates by 10 per cent against the dollar over the year, your money will have grown by 18 per cent in sterling terms. On the other hand, if you have guessed currency movements incorrectly, you will lose money.

At an early stage of saving and investment you will probably not want to speculate on currency movements. However, when you have a sizable portfolio, and a better feel for the markets, you may well want to keep a proportion of your cash in foreign currencies. Accounts can be opened through major banks, but be sure to shop around to keep account charges as low as possible – they tend to be much higher than for ordinary sterling accounts.

Another way of putting cash into foreign currencies is to use an offshore currency fund. Shares in the funds can be purchased through a broker or direct from the funds themselves, but you will be liable to tax on both capital gains from currency movements and from interest paid out. If you choose to invest in an offshore currency fund (outside the borders of UK jurisdiction), be very careful to pick only the biggest and best investment institutions, as your deposits will not be protected by the UK authorities in the event of a bust.

Key Points

- Keeping your money on deposit might seem safe and boring to the novice investor. But during periods of market turmoil and uncertainty, this is exactly what you will want from an investment.

- You can accumulate savings tax-free in a TESSA or National Savings account, and the power of compound interest will rapidly multiply your money.

- Ensure that your current account pays maximum interest. The interest earned can go straight into your investment plan.

- Avoid going into the red on your current account and having to pay interest and bank charges. If you plan and monitor your spending carefully this should not happen.

- Take advantage of interest-free credit rather than paying cash when buying major items.

- Cash holdings will be the bedrock of your investment plan, and are particularly appropriate when saving for the deposit on a house or some other large future purchase.

CHAPTER 7

Buying a House

Many people believe that buying a house will be their best-ever investment. Certainly it is likely to be their largest-ever purchase. Whether or not it is their best *investment*, which will rise steadily in value well above the rate of inflation, depends upon the point on the economic cycle at which the house is bought. Residential property tracks the progress of the economic long wave better than do most other investments.

If property is purchased just after a depression (in the 1940s and 1950s, for example) a steady increase in price, sometimes above the level of inflation, is virtually guaranteed. This growth will be punctuated only by short recessions. If, on the other hand, property is purchased near the top of the cycle, and especially at the end of the period of false prosperity (such as the 1980s), then the opposite will be the case. A lengthy period of falling prices will ensue, lasting a decade or so, bringing prices down from their euphoric peaks to levels more in line with what property can reasonably earn in rents, as compared with other investments.

There is no doubt that in our experience of the current long wave house prices have grown astronomically over the last 30 years, and in particular over the last seven years of the secondary prosperity, from 1982 to 1988. However, there are now serious doubts about the performance of housing as an investment, at least over the next decade. Prices have already fallen sharply in many areas over the past few years. This state of affairs was literally unthinkable for many people before the slump became reality. Almost everybody believed that houses could only appreciate in value – a classic example of the delusions of the majority close to the peak of a market.

Buying a house as a place to live in, rather than as an investment, is another matter entirely. In this chapter we shall consider both the 'investment' and 'utility' aspects of housing.

The Great Housing Myth

Let's start by taking a look at the still-widespread myth that buying a house at today's prices is a virtually guaranteed investment. This myth retains tremendous force in the popular imagination, and despite recent evidence to the contrary, the majority of people still believe that buying a house is the best long-term investment. Perhaps we should examine what is meant by the term 'investment' in this context, and attempt a rational assessment of the pros and cons of buying a house.

Probably the first aspect of the myth, which can be dealt with immediately, is the notion that subsidized mortgage funds are cheap. Certainly they are among the cheaper forms of borrowing, as you get tax relief on a relatively low level of interest, close to the base rate. However, we have already noted that in real terms interest rates are exceptionally high. During the high inflation of the 1970s it made sense to buy a house with cheap loans at interest rates which were actually *below* the rate of inflation. As the borrower's income rose he or she could repay the money in wages which were generally growing faster than the cost of borrowing. During the low-inflation 1940s–1960s mortgage interest rates were low, but not quite as cheap as during the high inflation period. Interest rates stood at 5 to 6 per cent for long periods, giving real returns to lenders of 2 to 3 per cent.

This equation was reversed in the 1980s, as inflation fell sharply and real interest rates rose to very high levels. Now borrowers found themselves chasing escalating mortgage rates and even faster increases in the price of houses. Yet such was the mass psychology of the boom that many late-comers persuaded themselves that they must jump on the housing bandwagon or forever be forced to rent. Experience since the puncturing of the boom in 1988 has forcibly damaged but not yet entirely dispelled this notion.

In the 1990s many borrowers have found themselves saddled with very large mortgages and very high borrowing costs. At the same time, wages growth is decelerating and unemployment is rising. For some people, wages are actually decreasing as bonuses and commissions are cut, or as wage freezes are negotiated.

The debt burden is high for home-owners as a whole. In fact, they are often paying far more to borrow money than to rent property. Few people in this situation have actually bothered to calculate the real costs of buying a house.

Let us take an example. The average house in this country currently costs £70,000. If you were to borrow the money to buy such a house – and could manage a deposit of £10,000 – then you would take out a mortgage of £60,000. At current rates this would

Table 7: The Real Costs of Buying a House

Borrowing costs at 12% p.a.	=	£6,876
Capital opportunity cost	=	£1,000
Insurance and maintenance	=	£ 350
Total	=	**£8,226**

cost 12 per cent a year, although recently the cost has been higher, and it could conceivably rise again in the future.

The monthly cost of borrowing at this rate will be £573. To this we must add the opportunity cost of capital tied up in the house. If your £10,000 deposit could earn 10 per cent per annum interest net of tax, this adds £1,000 per annum to the cost of borrowing. We should also add the cost of insurance and maintenance of the house, which is put conservatively at £350 a year, or .5 per cent of its capital value. The bill now looks as shown in Table 7.

Not included in this calculation are the extra costs of life insurance or mortgage protection insurance, ground rent if the property is not freehold, and service charges, which apply to some communal properties. All of these charges would add considerably to your bill. You might like to make a realistic estimate of the costs of buying your current property taking these variables into account. If you calculate that your home has appreciated in value since you bought it, then figure out the opportunity cost of the equity (the realistic market value of the house minus the mortgage).

If the person buying the £70,000 house in our example has an income of £20,000 (which would be necessary if he or she wanted to borrow a mortgage of £60,000, or three times income), then the house would be swallowing up 41 per cent of his or her gross (before-tax) income! The proportion of after-tax income eaten up by the house would be even larger, at over 50 per cent.

At present, it is still possible to rent property in many parts of the UK for much less than it costs to buy. Rents vary from 3 per cent of capital values in some country areas to about 8 per cent in some cities. The average is nearer 5 per cent. Assuming that the would-be property owner could rent a similar £70,000 house for 5 per cent of its value, then he or she would be paying £3,500 a year, with no insurance or maintenance charges to worry about. With a deposit of one month's rent, the bill looks as is shown in Table 8.

This produces an annual *saving* of £4,691 compared with the cost of buying. Therefore, in order for the house to be considered an investment, it must grow in value by at least 7 per cent a year in order to make up for the immediate loss it causes.

While it is certainly true that house price inflation has grown at more than 7 per cent a year during the false prosperity era of the

Table 8: The Real Costs of Renting

Annual Rent	=	£3,500
Opportunity cost of 10% deposit	=	£ 35
Total	=	**£3,535**

1980s, house prices began to fall towards the end of the decade and into the 1990s. As long as this trend continues, losses will be compounded. From an investment point of view, house prices should continue to fall until their yields from renting offer a reasonable rate of return (compared for example with deposit account interest rates), net of running costs such as maintenance and management fees, and of tax. At current interest rates this would require a yield of around 15 per cent, which implies that for the investor in residential property, prices will have to fall by a half to two-thirds, depending upon the type of property and the area in which it is located.

If you still wish to consider housing as an investment, you must take a very long-term view and trust that inflation will come to your rescue. Rents can be expected to rise broadly in line with inflation, whereas mortgage payments will be more or less steady, and will fall in real terms over time. With an inflation rate of 6 per cent per annum, a rent of £3,500 per annum will rise to £6,300 per annum after 10 years. In the example given above, this will approximately equal mortgage payments at 15 per cent of income, assuming that earnings grow at an average rate of 8 per cent per annum. From the tenth year onwards, therefore, mortgage payments should be cheaper than rents.

Buying a House as a Place to Live

Houses are not, of course, just pieces of property. If you are already living in a mortgaged house, or want to buy one, then you are likely to be or become emotionally attached to it. Not everyone wants to put up with renting, the insecurity of its tenure, and having to live with someone else's tastes in furniture and fittings.

Also, for the purchaser who wishes to live in the house, the point at which purchasing becomes economic is a little higher than for the investor in property – namely, where it is as cheap to buy as it is to rent. In the example above, this would mean a 50 per cent fall in prices. In some places (notably London) prices have already fallen considerably, narrowing or even eliminating the premium gap between buying and renting.

How Much Can You Afford?

The first thing to decide when searching for a house is how much you can afford to borrow. I would suggest that you make this a conservative figure, allowing a reasonable degree of leeway for other spending and leaving a margin to cover any possible future cuts in income, for example if you should lose your job. It is not a good idea to beggar yourself just to buy a house.

Traditionally, building societies have allowed maximum advances of up to two-and-a-half times income. This is for mortgages on which you would be expected to put down a deposit of at least 5 per cent and up to 20 per cent of the purchase price. During the boom years it became possible to get mortgages of up to four times income, and zero-deposit schemes were also on offer. Some mortgage brokers may still offer you these terms. These schemes usually penalize the higher-risk borrower with higher interest rates, however.

If two people are purchasing together, responsible lenders will normally allow the smaller of the two incomes to be added to the borrowing limits of the larger. So sensible borrowing limits in this case would be a maximum of 2.5 times the larger income plus 1 times the smaller. You should also be prepared to accumulate a deposit of at least 10 per cent of the purchase price. If you have already sold a property and are sitting on a pile of cash, I would suggest that you keep at least half of this money for your investment programme. You do not want to see all of your assets swallowed up in the black hole of falling property values.

Having established your borrowing limits and decided on the type of mortgage you require (see below), you will be able to obtain that mortgage and go shopping for a home. Having the mortgage already arranged will increase your bargaining power. You will have lots of choice, so take your time.

Probably the best strategy to adopt in a falling market is the scavenger approach. Ask the agents which properties are on their books which absolutely have to be sold, and scour the newspapers looking for distress sales or the dumping of unwanted inheritance properties. It may also be worthwhile to contact building societies to find out whether you can purchase properties upon which they have already foreclosed. Some building societies actually offer discounted mortgages to buyers of repossessed property. Don't forget property auctions, where much of this type of property ends up.

The game you will play is to see lots of houses and then to make offers which reflect both your borrowing limits and what you consider to be a reasonable price in relation to rental values. Many

of these offers will be rejected by owners and agents as 'cheeky',
as both parties will retain unrealistic views of what the property is
really worth. Eventually, however, you will come across individuals
or institutions who are anxious to sell and who will accept your offer.
There is no hurry – you are buying a house to live in, and you want
to pay as little as possible for it. So be persistent and be cheeky!

As the housing slump has deepened large variations in prices
have begun to appear, reflecting the differing requirements and
perceptions of sellers. Those who have to sell will produce the
'bargains', or rather, will reduce their prices to realistic levels. Those
who are not desperate to sell will keep their prices at unrealistic
levels hoping some fool will pay it. Usually these vendors will be
disappointed. Nevertheless, there are still lots of people who
believe that house prices are set to shoot up again and who may
consider that they are getting a 'bargain' by paying for a house that
costs them four times their income levels and twice the rental
premium.

Do not join this self-deluding band, who could easily become the
heavily mortgaged *nouveau pauvre*. Remember the important
ratios relevant to house purchase and keep up the bargain hunting.
You will eventually be amply rewarded.

Choosing a Mortgage

There are quite a variety of mortgages on offer at the moment.
Some are new financial products which were made available
during the profligate 1980s, such as pension mortgages, equity-
linked mortgages, and low-cost endowments. These are all
variations on the same theme, where you pay interest on the money
borrowed and sign up for an investment plan to accumulate a sum
of money sufficient to repay the borrowed principal.

Against these we have the traditional method of buying a home,
often denigrated as old-fashioned, known as the repayment
mortgage. Through this method you repay both capital and interest
over a length of time, which is usually 25 years but can be longer
or shorter depending upon your circumstances. As long as you can
keep up the repayments the debt will be repaid in full by the end
of the period.

The Costs of a Mortgage

Many people are keen to take on a mortgage, thinking only of the
maximum amount they can borrow and what this costs in terms of
a monthly payment. But it is worth calculating exactly how much it
will cost you to borrow the money. Table 9 gives examples of the
total costs of borrowing different lump sums for house purchases,

Table 9: Costs of Mortgages at 12 % p.a. over 25 Years

Sum Borrowed	Payments			Multiple of Principal
	Monthly	**Annually**	**Total**	
£ 30,000	£254.40	£ 3,053	£ 76,320	2.5
£ 50,000	£467.00	£ 5,604	£140,100	2.8
£ 75,000	£732.75	£ 8,793	£219,825	2.9
£100,000	£998.50	£11,982	£299,550	3.0

based on a straight repayment mortgage over 25 years, at an average interest rate of 12 per cent.

It can be seen from Table 9 that the amounts repaid are large. Even for a relatively small mortgage of £30,000 attracting full tax relief the sum repaid amounts to more than £76,000, some two and a half times the sum borrowed. The more you borrow, the greater is the multiple of the principal repaid. A large mortgage of £100,000 requires a repayment of almost £300,000, three times the original sum borrowed!

Of course, interest rates will vary over the life of the mortgage. In recent years they have been as high as 15 per cent and as low as 8 per cent. With a variable rate mortgage your monthly payments will move up and down in line with these changes. Whatever the rate, borrowing mortgage money will cost you a lot in the long run.

Reducing the Overall Cost of a Mortgage

The total cost of a mortgage is high because of the powerful effect of compound interest. You can reduce this effect considerably by repaying your mortgage over a shorter period. If you cut the repayment period in the example above from 25 years to 15 years, then the result will be as shown in Table 10.

It can readily be seen from Table 10 that the savings are considerable. If you can find the extra 20 per cent or so to add to your monthly repayment, buying a house on a 15-year mortgage means that you can repay the loan in 60 per cent of the normal time. That will give you an extra 10 years of rent-free living, and dramatically boost your future savings rate and standard of consumption.

If the idea of early mortgage repayment attracts you, then it can be easily arranged if you have a repayment mortgage. Simply ask your lender to recalculate the amount owing over a 15-year period (or 20 years, or 10, longer or shorter as you wish). There may be a small remortgage fee payable, and you should check if there are any early redemption penalties.

Table 10: Mortgage Repayment

Principal	Monthly	Annually	Total	Saving
£ 30,000	£ 310.20	£ 3,722	£ 55,836	£20,484
£ 50,000	£ 555.00	£ 6,660	£ 99,900	£40,200
£ 75,000	£ 861.00	£10,332	£154,980	£64,845
£100,000	£1,167.00	£14,004	£210,060	£89,490

It has to be said that some people seem to believe that it is a good idea to carry on paying an almost endless mortgage. Many financial advisers will argue that you should take advantage of the £30,000 mortgage tax relief in order to enjoy cheap borrowing. This is a valid argument only if you can be sure that guaranteed investments in cash or bonds will yield appreciably more than you are paying in mortgage interest net of tax. This is not often the case. Furthermore it assumes that you actually have the spare £30,000 to invest. For a person starting out with a mortgage this is unlikely to be the case.

It makes much more emotional and financial sense to own your home outright, and to do so as soon as possible. Given that housing costs are the greatest monthly burden for most households, the person with no mortgage has a tremendous financial boost. A key component of achieving financial independence has to include owning the roof over your head – provided that you have bought it at the right price and paid for it as quickly as possible.

Other Forms of Mortgage Repayment

Endowment Mortgages

The most common type of mortgage is the *endowment* mortgage. With this a borrower elects to pay interest for a given period, which is usually 25 or 30 years. The principal is repaid from an investment fund which is managed by the insurance company that issues the mortgage. The borrower takes out an endowment policy in order to make contributions to this fund. The fund should then grow to meet or exceed the principal of the loan over the period for which it is borrowed.

There are various types of endowment policy. Only guaranteed 'with profits' policies are certain to repay the sum assured. A type commonly sold is called the low-cost endowment, which will not usually *guarantee* to repay the principal. However, the performance of endowment funds over the long bull markets since the 1960s has been excellent, so that even low-cost endowments have produced handsome sums, often in excess of the principal to be repaid.

Hence the popularity of endowment mortgages in the 1970s and 1980s, when borrowers became convinced that extra profits were virtually guaranteed.

We have seen that investment carries few guarantees, especially when it involves heavy exposure to the stock-market. Unfortunately, low-cost endowments are unlikely to perform well over the next decade or so, unless their fund managers are exceptionally able. This will result in reduced profit expectations for holders of endowment policies. In some cases it could even mean that at the end of the term the investment fund is insufficient to repay the sum borrowed.

There is another important reason why endowment policies have been so widely accepted. They are sold by an army of investment advisers and employees of banks and building societies, who collect commissions for their efforts. On the other hand, commissions on repayment mortgages are likely to be small or non-existent. Often, you will need to insist quite strongly that you would prefer a repayment mortgage in the face of a salesperson keen on a commission. Many brokers deal only in endowment mortgages and other investment-related products, and will not be able to offer you a repayment mortgage.

Endowment mortgages have other drawbacks. The investment performance of the funds varies quite widely, so it is wise to check their records beforehand. Management charges will be levied on an annual basis as well as front-end commissions (charges made when you take out the loan). The investment funds may also have a front-end charge levied on your monthly instalments. All of these costs may be hidden in the small print, but they make the monthly premiums-plus-interest payments on endowment mortgages substantially higher than those for ordinary repayment mortgages.

There is yet another problem with endowment policies. It is difficult to realize the true value of your investment if you cash it in during the early years. If you are contemplating a move, you would do far better to renegotiate the terms of your existing policy than to cash it in. You would receive substantially less for your policy than the amount paid in, once commissions, fund management charges and policy administration fees have been deducted.

The cost of negotiating a short-term endowment mortgage is also likely to be much higher than with a repayment mortgage, as you would have to invest a much larger amount monthly on a with-profits basis to be sure of deriving a sum large enough to repay the loan. Thus endowments are better suited to long-term borrowing.

Having said this, there is no reason why an endowment mortgage cannot offer reasonable value if it is issued by a reputable company with a good track record of fund management, reasonable levels of management fees, and no propensity for forking out too much in commissions to intermediaries.

PEP and Pension Mortgages

These are variations on the endowment theme. With both you repay interest monthly, and make investments to pay off the principal. A PEP mortgage invests your money in a Personal Equity Plan, which is a portfolio of shares enjoying tax-free returns up to certain limits (see chapter 10 for more details). A pension mortgage again takes advantage of tax concessions (see chapter 8) to build up a lump sum, which is withdrawn on your retirement and used to repay the loan.

Pension mortgages can make sense if you choose a good investment company and if you are due to retire in the not too distant future (say 25 years). If you take out a pension mortgage when you are young and have 30 or more years to retirement, then you are paying extra interest and would be better off with an endowment or repayment mortgage.

PEP mortgages are not to be recommended. Running costs can be quite high, despite the tax concessions. And it would be foolish to trust the long-term security of a roof over your head to the vagaries of the stock-market. Use cash or low-risk investments to repay housing loans.

Foreign Currency Mortgages

These are currently in vogue, owing to the large differential between UK interest rates and those of other currencies. The most sophisticated ones offer the borrower managed loan accounts, where the outstanding sum is switched between currencies. Others offer investment only in one country's currency, or in the ECU (European Currency Unit), which is based on all the EEC currencies.

Foreign currency mortgages can offer good results – until exchange rate movements go against sterling, in which case the value of your outstanding loan can rise sharply. Some managed currency accounts can claim good results for their clients by switching in and out of currencies and hedging to minimize this risk. If you don't mind the risk, and have a financial cushion in case things go wrong, then a managed foreign currency mortgage arranged with a company with a good track record might be worth considering. However, if you are starting out on the road to home-ownership, and have little in the way of a financial cushion, they are not to be recommended.

Finally – Beware of Vested Interests!

In the UK there is more rubbish written and spoken about the housing market than any other market, with the possible exception of shares. The points of view that you hear are invariably those of estate agents or building society employees – people whose very livelihood depends upon the sale of lots of houses. Most of these professionals never dreamed that a residential property crash could happen, especially one on the scale recently experienced. Some have even quoted average national price changes, which are at best meaningless or at worst patently false, to disguise the true situation in the worst hit regions.

You are going to hear a lot more talk of the imminent upturn in the housing market and hopes of steadily rising prices once again. After all, vested interests have been predicting an imminent upturn ever since the crash began! Perhaps this could happen – if there were a substantial decline in interest rates, or a sudden explosion in rents that made mortgages look cheap once again. However, in many areas rents have been virtually static in money terms, and have fallen in real terms, throughout the years of the slump. This has occurred as more and more property has come on the private rental market. Interest rates have also fallen, which is to be expected during periods of economic decline, but they have not fallen enough to spark a sustained recovery in the housing market.

It is important to recognize that the vast majority of existing home-owners will hope for an upturn, and property professionals will fervently wish for it. But it will be a long time coming. The market is fundamentally distorted, and equilibrium will eventually be restored, mainly through a continued downward adjustment of house prices.

Key Points

- Housing has been a great investment for the past 30 years or so. Economic conditions have now changed fundamentally, so this is no longer true.

- Housing can be seen as an investment if prices are reasonable in relation to incomes and rents and if you can save rent by purchasing. You should not pay a large premium over rental value.

- If you are buying, establish tolerable borrowing limits and shop around. The market will continue to experience distress sales. Be a hard bargainer.

- Consider repaying your mortgage early by increasing your monthly payments if you are using the repayment method. You will save a great deal in interest charges.

- Understand the real costs of endowments. Renegotiate the terms rather than cashing in policies for less than their true values. Check the track records of the insurance companies undertaking the investments on your behalf.

- Assess pension mortgages in the same way as endowments. Avoid PEP mortgages. Understand the risks of foreign currency mortgages.

- Buy the right house, at the right price, using the mortgage that is right for you. Enjoy your 'investment' as an affordable place to live, irrespective of its future value.

CHAPTER 8

Pensions and Life Assurance

A pension is definitely one of the best investments you can make, although you do have to wait rather a long time before you are able to enjoy the fruits of your efforts! Many young people in their twenties or thirties take the view that a pension scheme is something that comes with the job and consequently does not deserve much attention, or that the future is so far distant that it is not worth bothering about making their own provision for a pension scheme.

At the same time, recent legislative changes have increased the range of choices open to would-be pensioners, causing some people to avoid the subject altogether or to put their trust entirely in pension company salespeople. Yet as always in financial matters, the basic choices are easy to comprehend once you have translated the jargon. Furthermore, it is absolutely imperative that you do provide for your future, and an efficient and reputable pension scheme should underpin your personal investment programme, guaranteeing you future wealth.

The State Pension

We hear a lot about the difficulties pensioners face when they receive only the income from a State pension. This is not surprising given its level of benefits. In 1991 the stipend was £2,704 p.a. for single people and £4,329 for married couples. Just compare this with your present salary and estimate whether you feel you could live adequately on it, even with the mortgage paid off!

Everybody is entitled to the basic State pension, which is index-linked annually to the rising cost of living. However, if you choose to defer taking your pension for a while, then its payment increases by approximately 7.5 per cent for every year of deferment. So it can make sense to defer taking a State pension for several years if you have enough money from other investments to subsist on at retirement.

The State also pays another pension, which is called SERPS – the State Earnings-Related Pension Scheme. SERPS currently pays up to £70 a week extra on top of the basic pension, although this will be reduced on a sliding scale after the year 2000. By the year 2010 the maximum benefit will be cut to only £56 a week.

If these sums of money seem small to you then you will be wondering how they might be boosted. The answer is to make sure that you are in a company pension scheme, or that you set up your own scheme. There are considerable government incentives open to those who are willing to provide for their own future rather than rely exclusively on the State.

The Tax Breaks

Pension schemes are fantastic investment vehicles for two main reasons. The first is that the money you pay into them is tax-free. This means that if you are a basic rate tax payer, when £100 goes into your pension scheme, £75 comes from you and £25 is handed over by the tax man. If you are in the higher tax band, then you only contribute £60, with £40 coming from the Inland Revenue. Your monthly contributions may appear to be quite small, but they grow rapidly with these extra payments.

The second major concession made by the Inland Revenue is to allow your pension fund to continue to grow free of tax right up until the time you retire. We have already seen from chapter 2 what compound interest can do to your savings. A few points extra on the interest rate makes a large difference to your savings over a long period. Your fund will be considerably larger when you come to retire than it would otherwise have been. Say, for example, that you save £100 a month (remember, this would only cost you £75 a month) for 30 years at an interest rate of 10 per cent per annum. Your pension fund would be worth £227,966 at the end of the period. Let us say that you save the same amount but it is allowed to grow at 13 per cent per annum, representing the tax concessions, over the same period. The amount accumulated would now equal £446,548 – almost double the taxed rate of interest.

So, you can save a relatively small amount each month, and have this augmented by the Government. The amazing power of compound interest will ensure that the fund grows rapidly to a very substantial sum. When the fund matures, you will be able to take a tax-free lump sum from it and then be assured of an income for the remainder of your life. Retirement may seem to be a long way off, but the investment rewards are very attractive!

Company Pension Schemes

Half of the work-force in this country is covered by company pension schemes. These vary in generosity. If you work for a large corporation or for the Government you will probably be in a scheme which rewards you on the basis of the number of years you have worked for them. For every year you work you will collect a proportion of your final salary. For example, if you work in the Civil Service you will be credited with 1/80th of your final salary for each year in which you are employed. If you work for 30 years, you will receive 30/80ths of your final salary, which is 37.5 per cent. So, for example, if your final salary were £40,000 per annum, your pension would be £15,000 per annum.

Many company schemes are 'non-contributory', meaning that contributions to the scheme are not deducted from your pay. Some require that a sum is deducted from your wages, which is added to by your employer. For example, you might contribute one-third and your employer two-thirds of the overall contribution.

You should be careful to find out what kind of pension you will receive at retirement. Some Government and large-corporation pension schemes pay out on an index-linked basis, meaning that your pension is increased every year in line with retail price inflation. This is a very valuable benefit. Unfortunately, these types of pension are in the minority. The majority will offer only a limited degree of index-linking, at 3 per cent a year, for example. If the inflation rate exceeds this, the real value of your pension will erode quickly.

If you think that your pension will not be large enough for your needs at retirement, or that it is insufficiently inflation-proofed, then you might like to consider making 'Additional Voluntary Contributions' (AVCs) of up to 15 per cent of your gross (pre-tax) salary, to either your company scheme or your own scheme. In the latter case, these would be known as 'Free-Standing Voluntary Contributions'. All this means is that a pension company sets up a fund for you to which you can contribute irrespective of your job.

With the company scheme, you will only be able to contribute while you are actually working for the company. The company scheme (which will be known as a group scheme) will probably offer the best terms overall, especially if it buys you more years of an inflation-proofed pension. However, the free-standing scheme has the advantage of flexibility.

Obviously, if you are in a company scheme this is good news for your overall investment programme. Many people are in these schemes but are not aware of their precise terms. You will need to contact your company's personnel office or human resources department to clarify exactly what your group scheme offers, so that you may decide whether to make additional contributions and on what basis to make them. The people dealing with pensions in your organization will be able to explain any of the technicalities or jargon which you might find puzzling.

Personal Pension Schemes

Personal pension schemes have recently been developed to offer maximum flexibility and benefits to the self-employed or to those employees who are not covered by group schemes. The Inland Revenue allows you to contribute a large proportion of your gross salary to a personal pension scheme. The exact amount depends upon your age, as you can see from the following table:

The figures in Table 11 represent large proportions of pre-tax earnings. It is unlikely that you will take advantage of all of them, unless you are earning a wage much higher than the national average. Nevertheless, if you are able to save up to the limit stipulated it is worth doing so in order to enjoy maximum tax advantages.

The Conservative Government overhauled personal pensions legislation in the late 1980s. As part of their package they offered a sweetener: If you opt out of SERPS when you start a personal pension scheme you will be credited with part of your National Insurance contributions plus tax relief on your pension contributions and a bonus amounting to almost 5.8 per cent extra going into your pension plan. The bonus is payable until April 1993.

All of these inducements mean that it is probably in the interests of relatively young people (say under 40) to opt out of SERPS. It is possible to rejoin at a future date – you might consider doing so 10 years or so before retirement in order to protect yourself from inflation to some extent. You should keep an eye out for changes in pensions legislation brought in by any future Government, which might put an end to this option.

If you are already in employment, then you can set up a free-standing scheme. This is similar to a personal pension plan in that it enjoys the same tax advantages, although it does not allow you to opt

Table 11: Allowable Contributions to a Personal Pension Scheme

Age	Percentage of Earnings Contributable up to £60,000
Under 36	17.5
36–45	20
46–50	25
51–55	30
56–60	35
61–74	40

out of SERPS. You can run a free-standing scheme alongside your company scheme in order to top-up your future pension income.

The choice of pension schemes is quite wide, but it is not particularly difficult to make a choice. As we have seen, all financial decisions should be defined by your personal circumstances. One thing is certain – unless you are in an exceptionally good group scheme and are confident of staying in the job until retirement, you will want to top up your existing pension arrangements. And if you are not in a pension scheme already, then you would be wise to take advantage of the generous tax concessions offered, as part of your overall investment programme.

How Much Should You Save?

The amount you will need to save will depend upon two key factors – the future rate of inflation and the future rate of growth of the savings in your pension fund. It is difficult to make predictions over a 30-year period, although we do have the long wave to help us as a general guide. We can assume, as the insurance companies themselves do, that a reputable pension fund will produce real rates of return at least 3.5 per cent above the rate of inflation, although there will be times when even the best companies find it difficult to meet this target, but also other times when they easily exceed it.

The point to consider is exactly how much money you feel you will need at retirement. You are allowed only to receive up to two-thirds of your final salary as a maximum. Let us also assume that you have paid off your mortgage and that your children are grown up. So you might anticipate that you could live very comfortably on half of your final salary.

Let us further assume that your final salary is going to be around £20,000 per annum in today's money, and that you will therefore need the equivalent of £10,000 per annum when you retire. The basic state pension (for a single person) can be deducted from this, leaving you with £7,300 to find. If retirement is 30 years off, and if inflation runs at an average of 5 per cent a year over this period, then your retirement income will need to be £31,550. You will need a pension fund totalling £315,500 in order to generate this income, assuming it produces a yield of 10 per cent annually.

If you are already in a company scheme, you will be relieved to hear that much of the burden of saving is lifted from you. If you are not so fortunate, then you would have to save £1,800 a year to achieve it, or 15 per cent of current income in the example. Perhaps you will only be able to save a part of this at first, increasing the amount as time goes on. But in order to accumulate the necessary final sum, you will need to start right away. It may seem difficult at first, but it will become easier as time goes on and your income rises to meet inflation.

Choosing a Pension Fund

How do you actually go about choosing a fund for your personal pension or free-standing scheme when there are so many to choose from? There are two main characteristics to look for. First, you will want to choose a fund which pays low commissions to intermediaries and which has low annual management charges. This will ensure that the maximum amount of money is invested on your behalf. Second, you will be looking for a fund which will perform well.

Most personal pensions are actually sold by intermediaries – that is, salespeople (who may call themselves brokers or financial advisers) who receive commissions from the insurance company that backs the pension scheme. The commission rates vary widely. If you are using an adviser, you must ask him or her what the rate of commission is for the recommended policy. Up to half of your first year's payments could go into the salesperson's pockets in the form of commission.

Another feature to look into is the management costs. Again, these vary widely. An efficient company will keep its management charges below 10 per cent of the premiums. A more profligate company could charge you over 30 per cent of the money you pay annually in premiums. So if you are using a broker you will again want to ask questions about these charges.

Next you will want to consider performance. Having chosen a company which invests the maximum amount of your premiums there is already a fair chance that it will be a good performer, as more of your money is put to work on your behalf. It is no surprise therefore that mutual funds are well represented in the lists of top-performing funds. These are companies which have no shareholders – instead, all the policyholders are mutual 'owners', and share out the profits accordingly. So another slice of money comes your way that would otherwise not have been available.

Performance tables are published in professional magazines such as *Planned Savings* and *Pensions Management*, and although past performance is not necessarily a guide to the future, it is the only guide we have.

A perusal of the performance tables will show that certain names crop up frequently in the top 20. Some companies stand out well above others in terms of their long-term investment record. It is wise to consider with-profits funds, which tend to give the best returns, and to investigate performance over a long period of 10, 15 or 20 years. Once you have made your choice, contact the company directly, thereby avoiding intermediaries' charges.

Life Assurance Plans

The area of life protection is one of the most confusing in terms of sheer jargon and the variety of plans offered. However, we can eliminate much of the confusion by identifying three basic types of life assurance:

1. term assurance
2. whole life assurance
3. endowment assurance

All three will pay out a lump sum in the event of your death. However, the costs of ensuring that lump sum can vary widely.

Term Assurance

This is the cheapest 'no-frills' assurance, and can be recommended. There are three variations on this theme. *Level term assurance* means that in return for your premium you get a set level of protection over a set period, for example, £100,000 to be paid out to your dependents if you should die at any time over the next 20 years. Of course, the real value of that £100,000 will erode over time due to inflation.

To overcome this problem you can take out *increasing term assurance*, whereby both the premiums and the assured sum increase each year. Alternatively, you can take out *decreasing term assurance*, whereby the premiums and sum assured fall each year. This type of assurance is often known as *mortgage protection assurance*, as it can be taken out to cover the decreasing amounts outstanding over the lifetime of a mortgage.

Whole Life Assurance

These policies are often called *permanent policies* because as long as you keep paying the premiums they will pay out at any time you may die, not just within a fixed period, as with term assurance. Because they are permanent they have a cash-in value, called a *surrender value*. But they are more expensive because you are paying for extra protection and because the money used is invested on your behalf by the insurance company. Two types of investment schemes are available:

1. with-profits whole life
2. unit-linked whole life

The with-profits system is like a with-profits pension fund. Each year a bonus is payable depending upon the performance of the fund. Once added the bonuses cannot be removed, although they are only payable on the death of the beneficiary. So the sum for which your life is assured rises automatically as the policy ages.

The unit-linked system is one in which your premiums are used to buy units in the funds managed by the insurance company. The value of your life assurance policy rises and falls with the current value of the units. If there is a stock-market crash, down goes the value of your life policy. They are therefore not recommended for the cautious investor.

Endowment Policies

These are basically investment schemes which are due to mature at a given date. Until maturity you enjoy life cover. At maturity your life cover ceases but you get a lump sum, the amount of which depends upon the performance of the fund in which your money has been invested.

Similarly to whole life policies, endowments can be structured on a unit-linked or with-profits basis. And as with pension schemes, you will want to be sure that the company investing the money on your behalf is doing so using the lowest possible administration charges, and you will want to pay as little commission as possible to brokers who may be acting for you. Although the investment performance of insurance funds may be disappointing compared to other savings vehicles, there is one large advantage with endowment policies – their proceeds are paid to you free of tax. This is one reason why endowment policies are popular forms of mortgage repayment.

As we have seen in chapter 7, there are variations on the endowment theme, such as low-cost endowments, which are expected to produce the required final sum necessary to repay a mortgage but do not guarantee this. Only guaranteed with-profits endowments will do this.

One very useful feature of endowment policies is that you can use them as security for borrowing. The life assurance company will lend you up to 80 per cent or so of the current value of the policy at very low interest rates – usually close to the prevailing mortgage interest rate. Thus, if you need money to make a large purchase, such as a car, borrowing against your endowment policy for short periods could save you money. Contact the insurance companies for full details of their particular loan terms and conditions.

How Much Life Assurance Do You Need?

With life assurance in general, the more you pay in premiums the more cover and/or contributions you make to investment plans. If you have no children, and if your partner is quite capable of earning a living without you, then there is no need to have life assurance at all.

If you work for a large firm, it is quite likely that you are already covered by a death-in-service benefit of 2 to 3 times your gross annual salary. If you are not covered, then you might like to suggest a life assurance plan to your employer.

If you have dependents, such as small children, then you will want to ensure that they will be provided for in the event of your premature death. However, there is no need to go overboard with this. Cover is only required until the youngest has grown up. So you might be looking for 20-year term assurance, for example, or for a 20-year endowment policy that will give you something in return for your regular premiums.

Remember that if a plan sounds too good to be true then it probably is! Life assurance premiums that incorporate a savings plan can be several times more expensive than plain term assurance. You might be better off investing the difference on your own account. Certainly the blandishments of commission-hungry salespeople should be subjected to the closest scrutiny – remember, the more expensive your life assurance scheme the heftier his or her commission probably is.

Key Points

- A pension scheme is a very powerful savings scheme, accumulating cash tax-free. If you are not in an adequate company scheme, then consider taking out a personal pension plan.

- The costs and returns of pension savings plans vary widely. Always shop around and ask about commissions, administration fees and long-term performance.

- If you are in a company scheme and want extra spending power at retirement, consider making additional voluntary contributions (AVCs) to either your group scheme or your own plan.

- Life assurance is a must for people with dependents. But don't burden yourself with inappropriate levels of cover in expensive investment schemes. Term assurance or low-cost endowments can be perfectly adequate.

CHAPTER 9

Bonds for Bears

We have seen in chapter 5 that there are three main investment vehicles - cash, bonds and shares. Cash has been discussed in chapter 6, so now we may turn our attention to bonds. You will remember that a bond is simply a piece of paper issued by a government, a company or a local authority which promises to pay a fixed amount of interest to the holder, usually for a fixed period of time.

Interest is paid on the face value of the bond, and is known as the coupon. Therefore, if you have a bond with a face value of £100 paying a coupon (fixed interest rate) of 10 per cent annually, you are guaranteed to receive exactly £10 a year in interest regardless of the market value of your bond.

The market value of your bond will rise and fall in line with changing interest rates. If interest rates fall, the value of your bond will rise. This happens because the coupon is fixed, so the value of the bond must increase to adjust to the new level. To take a simple example, if interest rates fall from 10 per cent to 9 per cent, your £100 bond should also yield 9 per cent. If the coupon is a fixed 10 per cent, then the price of the bond must increase to £111.11, because £111.11 × 9% = £10.

This means that if you buy bonds when interest rates are high you will make money when interest rates fall. This makes bonds exciting investments during economic slumps, when they can easily outperform cash and shares. This is why bonds are often for bears - people who believe that markets are about to fall.

There are a wide variety of bonds on offer, but for reasons of safety and liquidity (ease of buying and selling) it is best to stick to top-quality bonds issued by reputable governments and by major companies. Most UK investors will buy mainly UK Government bonds, so we will consider these first.

Gilt-edged Securities

UK Government bonds are also known as gilt-edged securities, or simply 'gilts', and they are incredibly safe. Your bank might go bust and take your uninsured cash with it, but the UK Government is highly unlikely to go broke and will always be able to meet its obligations. So if you want maximum security, gilts are great.

Gilts are issued by the National Savings Stock Register, which is based in Blackpool (see 'Bonds and Stock Office' in the Appendix for the address). You can buy and sell stock listed on the register simply by completing a form, available at any Post Office. Buying gilts in this way is very cheap. If you buy through a stockbroker it is likely to be quite a bit more expensive, with an added cost of around 3 per cent of the amount purchased. However, a broker can execute your order straightaway, whereas you will have to wait a few days for your postal application to arrive at the National Stock Register Office and be processed. But this should not matter a great deal, as gilt prices are not usually very volatile over short periods.

The time to buy gilts is at the point on the economic cycle where shares have exhausted their potential and the economy is moving into recession, or when you believe that there are other good indications of falling inflation and consequent falls in interest rates. You will already have moved into cash to avoid any potential slump in share prices and will hold this liquid position until interest rates show clear signs of peaking. At this point you will be moving out of cash and into gilts.

A good example was the situation in 1989/90. Interest rates peaked at 15 per cent and stayed there for nearly a year. Share prices started to look increasingly vulnerable as a recession started to develop. Canny investors were already out of shares and into cash, being very content to get up to 15 per cent on their cash balances. They then moved into bonds at the time of the UK's entry into the European Exchange Rate Mechanism (ERM), knowing that interest rates would have to fall as the recession deepened. Interest rates were already being cut rapidly in the USA, and it was only a matter of time before the UK would follow suit. Bond prices jumped while shares fell and cash began to look less attractive.

During the boom years of the middle 1980s many investors sneered at bonds, thinking them safe but boring. When interest rates are moving down sharply, however, bonds are anything but boring. We have already seen that every 1 per cent cut in rates adds about 10 per cent to the value of bonds. In 1982, when interest rates fell sharply, some bond investors made up to 50 per cent profits within a year.

Gilts come in three main categories, known as long-dated, medium-dated, and short-dated. If the outlook is a bit uncertain investors like to hold short-dated gilts, those which mature in 5 years or less. If investors are feeling bullish about bonds, they will buy medium (5 to 15 years) or long (more than 15 years) securities. The longer the time period to maturity, the more volatile will be the price of the bond. When interest rates are falling, investors will make more profit by buying and holding long-dated bonds. If the outlook is highly uncertain and interest rates threaten to rise, they will minimize potential losses by holding short-dated bonds.

The Yield Curve

If you read about gilts in the financial press you will notice a lot of mention given to the yield curve. The yield curve is simply a measurement of the difference between the prices of short gilts and those at the long end of the spectrum. If you run your eye along the yields listed in the newspaper you will see that they are higher at one end than the other.

Traditionally, the yield curve has been positive, that is, short-dated gilts have yielded less than long-dated ones (see Figure 3). This compensated investors for future uncertainty. However, towards the end of the 1980s an inverted yield curve appeared, where short yields were higher than long yields. This happened because current interest rates were very high and short-dated gilts were in direct competition with money-market funds.

When an inverted yield curve occurs it is very unusual and is a good indicator of an impending recession. Recessions are good for gilts, as interest rates will fall as the Government attempts to revive the economy. Investors will move into long gilts at this point, and eventually the yields at the short end will fall, causing the curve to flatten out.

Choosing Gilts

The type of gilt you choose to invest in will depend partly upon the degree of risk you want to take. It will also depend upon your tax position. If you are a non-taxpayer you will simply want to go for the best yields. However, if you are a taxpayer, then you will want to go for lower yields. This is because the income paid by gilts is taxable. It is paid gross if you buy direct from the National Stock Register, but you have to declare it on your tax form and you will pay tax at your normal rate. However, any capital gains you make from buying and selling gilts are not taxed. This makes astute trading of low-yield gilts particularly attractive to higher-rate taxpayers.

Interest payments are normally made twice a year, although

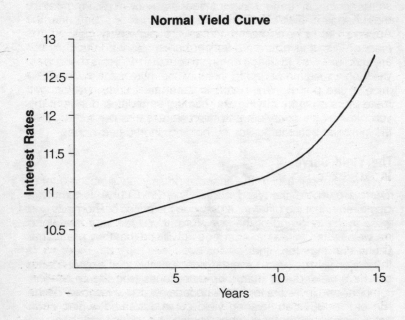

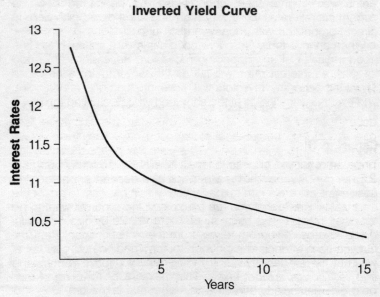

Figure 3: Yield Curves

some issues pay up four times a year. A full list of gilts of different maturities is available from the Bonds and Stock Office (see the Appendix for the address). Prices are published daily in the *Financial Times*, under the section marked 'British Funds'. Yields are calculated according to two measures. The first is the current yield (also called the running yield), which relates the coupon (the interest rate paid by the bond) to the market price. The second measure is known as the gross redemption yield, and simply tells you what the yield would be, at the current market price, if you held the bond until maturity .

Index-linked Issues

These are another form of gilt, introduced in 1982. The coupon is quoted in real terms, that is, allowing for inflation. Index-linked gilts will always pay the going inflation rate plus this real coupon, which makes them attractive in times of high or rising inflation. Conventional gilts have not always produced real rates of return. In the high-inflation 1970s, for example, gilts produced negative rates of return as they were unable to keep up with the rate of inflation.

Index-linked gilt prices are listed under the *Financial Times'* 'British Funds' section after the list of conventional gilts. The yields are quoted in real terms assuming two different levels of inflation – 5 and 10 per cent respectively. The actual price of an index-linked gilt is based on its market price plus retail price inflation as measured eight months previously.

Undated Issues

If you look at the list of gilts in the newspaper you will see half a dozen that are listed as 'undated'. These are the ultimate in long gilts in that they have no set redemption date. They were issued many years ago when interest rates were low, hence their very low price. An undated gilt with a face value of £100 and a coupon of 2.5 per cent will be trading at a price of around one quarter of its face value.

Undated gilts generally can be treated like long-dated stock in that their price is likely to be much more volatile than that of short-dated issues. There is always the remote chance that the Government will one day choose to buy the undated gilts back, while in the process of retiring Government debt. If this were to happen you would make massive capital gains, as the bonds would be repurchased at their face value. However, this is a very long shot indeed!

Gilt Unit Trusts

Another means of purchasing gilts is to do so through unit trusts. This method of investment is normally associated with shares, which are discussed in chapter 10. However, it is also possible to buy into trusts that specialize in gilts and other types of fixed interest investment, such as US Government bonds. They are listed under the 'Gilts and Fixed Interest' section of the unit trust performance tables, which you will find in financial magazines such as *Money Management* and *Money Observer*.

The advantage of unit trusts is that they are managed by professionals who use your money to buy and sell a broad portfolio of gilts to suit the circumstances of the market. The professionals should be able to milk that little bit more performance out of your portfolio than you might be able to get through more static investment. Unit trusts will either specialize in short-dated stocks or go for growth by purchasing longer-dated issues, so you can still pick your general strategy.

An attractive feature of some gilt unit trusts is that they charge low or even zero entry fees. The annual management charge will be 1 per cent or less, and the spread – the difference between unit buying and selling prices – should be low, at around 2 or 3 per cent. This compares with entry fees of 5 or 6 per cent for share-based unit trusts, with spreads of up to 5 per cent and management charges on top of this.

Unit trust selection is discussed more fully in the next chapter. For now you may like to note that it is wise to pick funds with a reasonable performance history as well as low entry fees and management charges. The funds with the lowest costs often feature at the top of the performance tables anyway, as more of your money is going into investment rather than into the pockets of the fund managers.

Foreign Bonds

Just as you might like to keep some of your cash in foreign currencies to take advantage of exchange rate fluctuations, so you might want to lock into high foreign interest rates by purchasing bonds denominated in foreign currencies. These have the added possibility of extra gains if their currencies strengthen against sterling.

It is fairly easy to find unit trusts which specialize in foreign bonds. The cheapest funds are those which concentrate on US Treasury bonds, which are the equivalent of our gilts. There is a massive market in these as the USA has been on a huge borrowing binge to finance its deficits. Funds such as the Whittingdale US Short-

Dated Bond and Beckman International Capital Accumulator have low entry charges, and are worth considering. Alternatively you can buy US Treasury bonds through a broker.

It is rather more difficult to find unit trusts which deal with other foreign fixed-interest markets which do not charge the usual 10 per cent or so in front-end fees, management fees and spreads. For this reason, if you want to buy bonds denominated in Deutschmarks, Swiss Francs or Yen it may be worth considering doing so through a broker, unless you only have small sums to invest and are taking the long view. Bonds in which you may be interested are listed in the *Financial Times*. It is best to choose those issued by governments or by really solid international agencies, such as the World Bank. Alternatively you can consider blue-chip companies which are unlikely to go under.

Junk Bonds

These achieved notoriety during the manic 1980s when firms like Drexel Burnam Lambert (now defunct) made massive fortunes out of them. They are bonds which pay exceptionally high interest rates and which are issued by companies raising money for expansion or acquisitions. They pay a high interest rate because they are high risk. During the current slump several of the bond issuers have found themselves unable to meet the interest payments on the bonds, and some have even gone into receivership.

Junk bonds are not therefore recommended for a conservative investment programme. You would have to be very confident of a company's prospects of survival to buy them during the current slump. However, if there are signs of a genuine upturn in economic prospects junk bonds could become undervalued and may be worth a small punt.

Third World Bonds

The Third World accumulated massive debts in the 1970s and 1980s, debts which it will never be able to repay. Some countries such as Brazil and Argentina have already effectively defaulted and are unable to pay the interest on their debts. Many banks have been forced to write off large chunks of their loans to these countries, and are refusing to lend them any more money. The Third World is bearing the brunt of the global slump, and further defaults can be expected.

As for corporate junk bonds, there is an active secondary market for third world bonds, where the paper is traded well below its face value. However, at least some of this paper is likely to end up decorating the mantelpiece, as did Tsarist Government bonds of the early 20th Century. Unless you are very confident and willing to learn a lot about this specialist market, it is wise to steer clear of such a high-risk area of bond trading.

Local Authority Bonds

Until recently, it was possible for the small investor to purchase bonds issued by UK local authorities. The most popular were the 'Yearling Bonds', which paid a fixed rate of interest over a whole year.

Unfortunately, few local authorities now issue bonds on their own account, as most of their cash now comes from central Government, which if it needs extra money can raise it from issues of gilts. The local authority bond issues that do remain tend to be traded in large amounts (£100,000 or more) and are not therefore accessible to the small investor. However, it is worth keeping an eye on the financial press for any signs of Yearling bonds returning to the market.

Convertibles

The last major type of bond to consider is convertibles. As the name suggests, convertible gilts are short-dated bonds which can be converted at some future time into longer-dated issues with a fixed price. They are useful for hedging your bets. If you believe that the gilts market is going to boom but are nervous about buying long gilts directly because of their volatility, you could buy a short-dated convertible. At a later date you could take up the option to switch when long prices have risen, only you will be buying in at a lower price.

Of course you will pay extra for the privilege of owning a convertible gilt. Whether you think it is worth the additional cost will depend upon its current price and the outlook for the market as a whole. Because of their hedging characteristics, convertible gilts are more likely to feature in the investment portfolios of professional fund managers than those of private investors.

Another type of convertible is a bond issued by a company which will be repurchased by the company at some future date. In the meantime it can be exchanged for a set number of shares at certain fixed dates, which are established by the company. In this case the investor is hoping that the price of the convertible will eventually be below the price of the shares, enabling him or her to make an immediate capital gain. The convertible will be priced above the current price of the shares, but occasionally the premium will narrow and investors may jump in to take advantage of the opportunity. Again this is quite a sophisticated strategy and may not be to the taste of all investors.

Your Bond Strategy

There is a distinct role for gilt-edged securities in your investment strategy. When interest rates have peaked and are on the way down you can enjoy substantial capital gains and have the added benefit of complete safety at a time when shares are likely to be performing poorly and when cash is looking less attractive.

The long wave tells us that the 1990s are likely to be good for bonds if share prices go down and stay down. During the last depression the return on shares was higher than that on gilts, reflecting the added risk of investing in shares. During the boom years this relationship reversed, with shares yielding less than gilts. This situation is known as the *reverse yield gap*. For example, the share market as a whole might give a 5 per cent return (yield), whereas gilts produce 10 per cent. A depression should make this gap disappear and re-establish the old relationship between bonds and shares.

Investors who moved out of cash and into bonds in 1990/91 will already be experiencing success as a result of this strategy. Good quality bonds are likely to experience a renaissance for much of the remainder of the decade. While you will be keen to move into shares in time for the next upturn, a basic portfolio of gilts is always a useful hedge against economic uncertainty.

Key Points

- Gilts are a good buy when interest rates are about to fall or are in a clear downward trend. Buy them through the Post Office to save broker's fees.

- Some unit trusts specialize in gilts and can give good returns if they have low entry charges and reasonable spreads between the buying and selling price.

- When sterling is falling relative to other major currencies it may be worth considering investment in foreign currency bonds backed by reputable issuers. Careful attention should be paid both to interest rates and to currency fluctuations should you do this.

- Junk bonds issued by heavily-indebted companies or countries should be avoided. Only if a firm economic recovery is underway could these bonds be considered undervalued. Stick to quality during a slump.

CHAPTER 10

Shares for Bulls

Following the Second World War, the 'cult of the equity' was born. It grew slowly at first, then gathered pace, and finally became frantic during the frenzied bull market of the 1980s. At such times the best possible investment seems to be in shares rather than bonds or cash. Investment advisers and stockbrokers point to the massive gains made from share investment since the 1950s and argue that this will continue evermore. Much of the investment of pension funds, unit trusts and the like continues to be in shares.

Shares are not always a good investment, however. The long upswing since 1940 has contained some pretty brutal bear markets, notably 1973/74 when shares fell in value by over 75 per cent; and the famous crash of October 1987 when shares lost nearly a quarter of their value in only two days! Optimists will tell you that these aberrations do not matter, as in both cases growth resumed and, over the long term, money continued to be made. Yet in recent years we have been in the grip of a bear market which has eroded these gains.

Nevertheless, the current bear market will eventually end, and savvy investors should be ready to buy up shares at bargain basement prices. It is precisely at the bottom of a bear market that things seem to be at their worst. It is very difficult to buy when all around you people are crying doom and gloom. It is easier to sell at the top and take a certain profit rather than to buy at the bottom when it might seem that there could be further losses. But this is what you must do. Remember the old Will Rogers saying: 'All you have to do to make money in the stock-market is to buy when shares are cheap and sell when they are dear'!

There are two important tools to help you to decide when shares are cheap and when they are dear. The first is *key ratios*, which can easily be monitored. The second is our old ally the long wave, which explains the general investment context.

Types of Shares

Companies can issue *preference* shares and *ordinary* shares, as well as more complicated securities such as *convertibles* and *debentures*. For most investment purposes, it is the ordinary share, or 'equity', that is of interest. This is simply a certificate issued by a company which represents a piece of the company itself. Any profits which the company makes will be distributed among the holders of ordinary shares, once its other commitments have been taken care of. These other commitments might include preference shareholders, who get a guaranteed fixed dividend, and owners of debentures, or loans made to the company which pay fixed rates of interest for fixed periods, like bonds.

Companies themselves are divided into different classes, reflecting their size and status in the market-place. The biggest and best are the *alpha* shares, which are also called 'blue-chips'. Next come the middle-ranking companies, which are designated *beta* shares, having shares in these companies is slightly more of a risk. Finally there are the small companies that carry the highest risk of unprofitability or outright failure and are known as *gamma* shares. Many of these will have share prices measured in pennies rather than pounds, so they are sometimes called 'penny shares'. Some of these represent once-large companies that have fallen out of favour; others are bright new flames which will one day make big profits. The difficulty lies in distinguishing one from the other!

If you want to make profits in the stock-market, it is better to stick to alpha and beta shares rather than to go for high-risk gamma shares. Within these first two categories there is still plenty of choice. It is best to take a long view of ordinary shares – you will buy to hold rather than frequently buy to sell. There are other ways of getting thrills and quick profits from the market, as we shall see in chapter 11, which deals with market speculating.

Valuing Shares

There are two common ways of measuring the performance of shares. The first is known as the *price/earnings* (or *P/E*) *ratio*. This is simply the price of the share divided by the total earnings of the company per ordinary share. Thus, if the price of a share is 100 pence, and its earnings are 5 pence, then the price/earnings ratio is 100/5, or 20.

The second important measure of the performance of a share is its *dividend yield*. The yield is simply the dividend expressed as a percentage of the share price. If a share is unpopular it will have a low P/E ratio and a high yield. If it is popular then it will have a high P/E ratio and a low yield. A recent example of this is bank

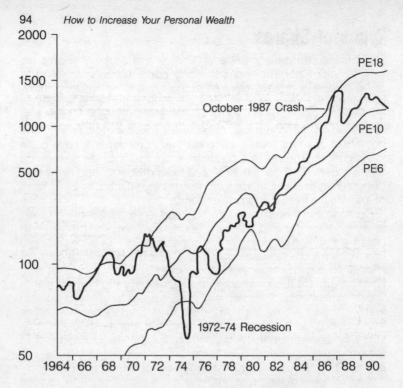

Figure 4: P/E Ratios and the Share Index Compared.
(Source: *Daily Telegraph*)

shares. These fell out of favour in 1990, and by the end of the year were yielding nearly 8 per cent, with average P/E ratios of 6. More popular sectors, such as food retailing, yielded closer to 3 per cent and had average P/E ratios of 13. Of course, these averages do not show the considerable variations of share yields and P/E ratios within the sectors.

In 1990, banks were unpopular because of growing fears of bad loans and falling profits. Investors could not accept that this situation would improve in the foreseeable future. On the other hand, food stores were seen as good defensive stocks in a recession, as people still have to eat whatever the state of the economy.

While it is possible to consider the condition of individual companies or sectors, it is also possible to measure the P/E ratio and dividend of the market as a whole. At the peak of a boom, such as in 1986/87, the overall P/E ratio is exceptionally high, at around 18 to 20, and the overall yield is low, at around 3 per cent. At the bottom of the worst of bear markets the P/E ratio is nearer 5, and the dividend yield more like 10 to 12 per cent.

Figure 4 shows how P/E ratios have changed between 1964 and 1990. You can see how large profits could be made from buying shares at the bottom of the trough in 1974/75 and selling them at the peak in 1987. There were of course some troughs on the way up, notably in 1976 and 1979. But in general the ride was very profitable.

Relating the market as a whole to what we know about the Kondratieff wave and Elliot wave theory as discussed in chapter 4, we can expect another major fall which will bottom out in the early 1990s. At this point overall P/E ratios should be down to 8 or less, with dividend yields up to 7 per cent or more. This will be the time to start buying shares in anticipation of the next big upward move.

It is possible to value the market as a whole by looking at these key indicators and relating them to your own perceptions of the outlook for the economy. You can follow the valuations of individual shares and sectors or the market as a whole by consulting the financial pages of any quality newspaper – the *Financial Times* giving the most detailed information. Detailed market comment is available from many sources, including daily and Sunday newspapers, business programmes on radio and TV, and specialist magazines such as *Investors Chronicle*.

A point to be stressed about share investment is that it should be seen as fairly long-term. You will need first to have money tucked away in cash and bonds for emergencies or buying a house. Share investment is risky, especially in the middle of a bear market, such as we may still be experiencing as you read this book.

The way to beat the risk is to pick safe shares which are good performers. Profits are not guaranteed, nor is the survival of the companies in which you invest, particularly during a slump. You will need to diversify, that is, to hold shares in several different companies at once.

Buying Shares

There are various ways of buying shares. If you have quite a lot of money to invest you can consider buying direct, through a stockbroker. This is not a good route for bargains of less than £500 or so, as you will pay commission of £20 or so on each deal you make. If you do have this kind of money to invest, however, then all you need to do is open an account with a broker, and thereafter telephone him or her with your investment requirements. You will be issued with a contract note, which will be followed by the share certificate itself – keep this in a safe place. The price you pay will be the one quoted to you by the broker on the day the bargain was struck.

Assuming that you don't have say £10,000 with which to buy 20 different shares, but still want to participate in a rising stock-market, then there are other avenues to consider. These include unit trusts, investment trusts, and personal equity plans.

Unit Trusts

These are an automatic choice for many beginners to the stock-market for the simple reason that they are heavily advertised and much discussed in the financial press. A lot of advertisements claim that unit trusts out-perform money placed in a building society account over 10 or 20 years' time. While this may have been true of the great bull markets of the 1970s and 1980s, it remains to be seen whether performance of this kind will be produced over the next couple of decades.

There is no doubt that unit trusts allow you to participate in share-purchase with relatively small amounts of money, and that they let you spread your risk by buying into a diversified share portfolio. Some even operate savings schemes so that you can invest a fixed monthly amount, even as little as £25 or so.

Unfortunately, unit trusts are expensive. An initial charge of 5 to 6 per cent is usually levied, and on top of that the spread – the difference between buying and selling prices – is often wide, at 5 to 7 per cent. There will also be an annual management charge of 1 per cent or even more. With this kind of fee structure you will need to make around 12 per cent on your first year's investment just to get your money back! So if you do buy unit trusts you should buy and hold onto them for the long haul – several years at least.

Prices are listed daily in the *Financial Times* under the heading 'Authorised Unit Trusts'. You will see offer (buying) and bid (selling) prices listed, with an indication of the current yield of the funds. In addition there will be a cancellation price listed, which is the lowest price at which the units can be sold. Quite a number of trusts deal only on a forward-price basis, meaning that when you buy or sell you pay or receive the price recorded the next time the unit trust portfolio is valued.

You will see from the *Financial Times* that there are an awful lot of unit trusts on offer – over 1,400 in all – so how do you go about selecting the ones that are right for you? The first thing to do is to get hold of a copy of a personal finance magazine (available from a good newsagent) such as *Money Management*, *Money Observer*, or *Planned Savings*. There you will find unit trusts listed by sector. There are 21 different sectors (see Table 12).

Table 12: Unit Trust Sectors

1. UK General – income plus capital growth
2. UK Growth – capital growth is the major objective
3. UK Equity Income – investing in high yield shares
4. UK Balanced – split between equities and gilts
5. Gilt and Fixed Interest – investing in UK bonds
6. Convertibles – investing in convertible bonds and gilts
7. Investment Trust Units – buying shares of investment trust companies
8. International Growth – international equity investment
9. International Equity Income – high yield from UK and foreign equities
10. International Fixed Interest – investment in international bonds
11. International Balanced – a mixture of equities and bonds
12. Funds of Funds – investing in other unit trusts
13. North America – investing in North American Securities
14. Europe – investing predominantly in European markets, including the UK
15. Japan – investment only in Japanese securities
16. Far East including Japan – the Japanese content must be less than 80%
17. Far East Excluding Japan – 80% of assets in Far Eastern markets
18. Australasia – concentrating on Australia and New Zealand
19. Commodity and Energy – oil, minerals, soft commodities and gold
20. Financial and Property – investing in companies only in these sectors
21. Money Markets – aiming to secure the best returns for cash

First you must select the sectors that you think will do well in the next few years. For example, if you feel that oil companies might profit from the next upwave, you will turn to the section marked 'Commodity and Energy'. There you will find over a dozen trusts which specialize in this general area. You can then compare the performance of each fund with its fellows. While past performance is not a firm guide to the future, it is the only indication you have. You can pick the most consistent performers on this basis. Alternatively, you could adopt the contrarian viewpoint and pick the worst performers on the grounds that they can only improve! Both systems have their supporters.

When you have identified the trusts that interest you, their entry and management costs can be compared. Obviously you will want to pay the lowest charges, other factors being equal. The charges are listed in the pages of the *Financial Times*. The *Financial Times* is also a useful source for the addresses and telephone numbers of the trusts so that you can send off or ring them for further information. It is well worth reading the prospectuses of the funds that interest you to ensure that you agree with the outlook and strategy of the fund managers.

These methods make the task of fund selection much easier, and if you like a little bit of detective work they can be a lot of fun! It certainly is important to do the task yourself rather than relying on a commission-driven adviser or an advertisement in the newspaper, which might be a touch misleading. It is your hard-earned money and it is up to you to invest it to optimum advantage.

Investment Trusts

These are one of the investment world's best-kept secrets. They are like unit trusts in that they hold diversified share portfolios in a number of different sectors (see Table 13). But they are not trusts, they are companies in their own right. As such, investment trusts have a share price and are bought and sold on the stock-market like the shares of any other company.

Table 13: Investment Trust Sectors

There are thirteen sectors identified for Investment Trusts. They are similar in composition to those identified for Unit Trusts. The sectors are as follows:

1. Capital and Income Growth: General
2. Capital and Income Growth: UK
3. Capital Growth: General
4. Capital Growth: International
5. Capital Growth: North America
6. Capital Growth: Far East
7. Capital Growth: Japan
8. Capital Growth: Commodity and Energy
9. Capital Growth: Technology
10. Income Growth
11. Smaller Companies
12. Special Features
13. Split Capital Trusts

For further information, contact: Association of Investment Trust Companies (see the Appendix for the address).

Investment trusts are immediately valuable because they usually trade at a price below the collective value of all the shares in their portfolio. In other words, their 'Net Asset Value' (NAV) is greater than the market price. This can be of little importance, unless the sector in which they are investing suddenly becomes popular, at which point they then trade at a premium to the NAV, above it. This happened for example in 1989/90 when investment trusts specializing in European shares suddenly became popular following the wave of liberalization in Eastern Europe. The value of an investment trust can also jump if it becomes a candidate for takeover by another company. Again this happened fairly recently when the British Coal Pension Fund acquired Globe Investment Trust and paid close to full value for it.

Another tempting feature of investment trusts is that they are much cheaper for the investor. Entry charges are low, the bid-offer spread is only around 2 per cent, and management charges are generally half those of unit trusts. Lower charges help to boost the performance of the trusts so that they can easily outperform unit trusts, especially in a bull market.

It is not difficult to find out more about investment trusts or to buy into them. The Association of Investment Trusts (see the Appendix) publishes monthly performance tables, as do financial magazines. Many trusts offer regular savings schemes to tempt the small investor. In fact, the sector is beginning to adopt a higher profile in an attempt to win business from the unit trusts. Investment trusts can be highly recommended as appropriate vehicles for share investment for the small investor – provided that the economic climate is correct for share investment.

Personal Equity Plans

Another method of share investment which is worth considering is a PEP. These were introduced by the Conservative Government in an attempt to encourage wider share ownership. They offer tax incentives, including the feature that all share dividends and capital growth accumulate tax free. The downside is that like unit trusts they can be expensive to set up and manage.

A recent survey of 230 PEPs found that the majority did not allow self-selection of shares. Those PEPs that do allow you to select the shares in which you want to invest may restrict the variety and the number of possible shares you may choose. However, some self-select schemes work out quite a lot cheaper than fully-managed PEPs.

PEP charges are generally similar to those for unit trusts. You should also beware of added dealing costs if you or the managers indulge in frequent switching of shares. This can eat into your profits. Another potential trap to beware of is double charging, if for example your PEP invests in unit trusts or investment trusts. It would be very damaging to have to pay both PEP charges and trust charges, so it is important to be clear as to whether you will be charged twice.

If you shop around for a PEP with a low level of fees – preferably one where you can operate a buy-and-hold strategy with good quality blue-chip shares – there is no reason why you should not do well over a 5 to 10 year period, particularly if you invest at the bottom of the bear market and ride the next upwave. PEPs have suffered recent losses in the downwave, which may have upset some existing investors.

The maximum you are currently allowed to invest in a PEP is £6,000 in any one tax year, or double this for a couple. A further £3,000 per person may be invested in the shares of a single company. This latter concession is of particular use to people who receive shares from their employers as part of an incentive scheme. This should be plenty for most people starting a share investment programme. You are also allowed to invest up to £3,000 in European Community shares. The PEP allowance is in addition to the normal £5,500 capital gains tax allowance available to investors. You may be tempted to use up this allowance first by purchasing shares directly rather than jumping straight into a PEP.

Friendly Society Schemes

Another good way to get started on a share investment programme is to buy into one of the Friendly Society schemes which are listed in the financial magazines. A special Government concession allows you to put up to £18 a month tax-free into approved Friendly Society schemes over a 10-year period. Societies usually offer a mixture of funds, with different weightings of shares and gilts. Performance is likely to be slow but steady, accumulating a useful sum over a decade. It is within virtually everybody's capability to tuck away such a small monthly sum.

Your Share Strategy

As the 1990s progress we find ourselves deep into the severe bear market predicted both by long wave analysis and Elliot Wave theory. Soon it will be time for the current 'pessimists' (who are in fact realists) to become optimists. There will be fantastic gains to be made for people who have the courage to buy shares when the market hits rock bottom. We will know when this point has been reached as the majority of investors will be avoiding shares, having experienced devastating losses. There will be widespread doom-and-gloom stories in the press, high unemployment, corporate bankruptcies and the like. Just such a situation occurred in 1974/75, and also, for those with long memories or a knowledge of economic history, in 1932. Remember the Rothschild maxim: 'The time to buy is when blood is running in the streets.'

Lurid as Rothschild's phraseology may be, it points up the advantage of following the long wave strategy and husbanding cash and bonds ready for the upturn. If you are a new investor, so much the better. You are about to make yourself a small fortune. Be ready to buy when the P/E and dividend ratios tell you so, and when the news is bleakest. Always remember to sell in good time next time the market goes off the rails – that is when the majority of investors once again become euphoric about shares. But that time is some way off.

Key Points

- Shares are not always a good investment. Pay attention to P/E ratios and yields in the market as a whole to decide when to buy and when to sell.

- Diversify your holdings. Buy unit or investment trusts if you are a small investor, so that you automatically invest in a diversified portfolio.

- Always be aware of the costs of buying through unit trusts and PEPs. Find schemes which charge the least and have reasonable track records.

- Make investment trusts the cornerstone of your share-buying programme if you are a small investor. Historically they have outperformed unit trusts.

- Take the time to learn about industrial and commercial trends so that you can anticipate sectors which will do well in the future. Use your library and read the financial pages of your newspaper.

- Trust your own judgement. Majority opinion is always wrong at major market turning points. Buy good quality shares and hold onto them for a number of years to gain the maximum advantage.

- Buying and selling shares at the correct time can make your fortune. Do not be afraid to buy when the P/E ratios and yield indicators tell you that the market is at rock bottom. The early 1990s should mark one of these historic turning points.

CHAPTER 11

Speculating to Accumulate

A programme of careful investment in cash, bonds and shares purchased and held at the appropriate times will build your wealth steadily. But you may feel impatient and get the urge to enter the murky waters of speculative investment. Perhaps you have heard of fortunes being made in financial futures and options trading, or from the astute buying and selling of commodities. This does happen, of course, but such 'investments' are for the average investor more in the nature of gambling.

That said, if you are willing to specialize and to learn about forms of speculative trading which are of particular interest to you, then there is no reason why you should not play the game, risking only the capital you can cheerfully afford to lose. If you do so, it must be with the knowledge that you can lose all the money, and in some cases *more than* all the money, that you have originally invested. This is because speculative investment employs the power of *gearing*, otherwise known as leverage. In effect this means using borrowed money, which dramatically increases gains, but amplifies losses.

I will discuss three main types of speculative investment: trading in gold and other precious metals, futures, and options. Of the three, buying and holding gold can be the least risky, and given the nature of today's economic climate circumstances may arise that will lead you to consider gold seriously.

Why Buy Gold?

Gold doesn't pay interest, unlike cash, bonds or shares do. It just sits there, fluctuating in value. So why bother to invest in it? The main reason is that gold remains the ultimate measure of value. Paper money is just so much paper if the government backing it is not careful to maintain confidence in the value of its banknotes. As recently as the 1960s the world financial system was hooked up to the gold standard, a system which had continued for several centuries – give or take the odd hiatus, usually brought about by the need to borrow for warfare.

Under the gold standard each currency had a fixed exchange rate. Without going into too many technical details, the gold standard ensured a tremendous degree of financial stability and confidence in internationally-traded currencies. In theory at least, you could exchange the currency note in your pocket for its equivalent in gold on demand. If a country imported too many goods, the value of its currency would fall, and it would be forced to sell gold to meet its obligations. This would cause the errant nation to import less, and its gold reserves would rise again. An automatic economic stabilizer resulted.

During the 1960s and 1970s governments began persistently to overspend. This was particularly the case with the USA, faced with the escalating costs of fighting the Vietnam war. The gold standard did not allow governments to run large deficits without depreciating their currency, so it was replaced with a system of free-floating currency exchange rates. This system works fine as long as everybody has lots of confidence in the major reserve currency. In the heyday of the British Empire the major reserve currency was the pound sterling, but between the First and Second World Wars it was replaced by the American dollar. During the depths of the depression of the 1930s, in a successful attempt to restore monetary stability, the dollar was hooked to gold at a fixed rate of $35 per ounce.

Gold rose steadily but unspectacularly in value from the 1930s until the last years of rapid inflation in the 1970s, when fears for the value of paper money caused it to leap in value. Over 1979/80 gold jumped from $300 per ounce to over $850. After this peak it subsided again to its current trading range of around $350 to $450. Sudden political crises which threaten economic damage can also affect the price of gold. Following the invasion of Kuwait by Iraq, the price of the yellow metal shot up by 20 per cent in less than a week.

In the modern world, gold is therefore best viewed as a hedge against uncertainty. A world economic crisis, fears over the strength of the dollar, or a prolonged slump can all lead to a jump in its price. For this reason, many people with larger portfolios like to keep 5 per cent or so of their assets in gold regardless of its current price. This holding is a form of insurance, to fall back on if all else fails. There are even extremists, known as 'gold bugs', who distrust all forms of paper money and hold as much gold as possible. They believe that the world is digging itself ever deeper into a financial hole through excessive borrowing and that one day in the near future all currencies will be forced back onto the gold standard.

How to Buy Gold

There are several ways in which you can buy gold. One of the simplest is to purchase gold coins through a bank. There are many different kinds in circulation, some of which are well-known, such as the Canadian Maple, the South African krugerrand and the British sovereign. It is quite easy to purchase gold in this way, and the coins have a ready market value. However, VAT is charged on gold coins, at the usual rate of 17.5 per cent.

Another way of buying gold is to do so indirectly by purchasing shares in gold-mining companies. These should be chosen using the techniques applicable to normal share selection, with careful attention paid to the stature of the company, its yield and the price/earnings ratio of its shares. Gold-mining companies are listed in the financial press under 'Mining'.

Alternatively, and of more applicability to the small investor, there are unit trusts which specialize in gold-mining companies. About a dozen are listed in the performance tables of financial magazines, under the 'Commodity and Energy' sector. These unit trusts should be analyzed and selected in the usual way, as discussed in chapter 10.

Finally, you can buy gold through a commodity broker and hold it in one of two types of account, known as allocated or unallocated accounts. With an *allocated* account you will be credited with title to an actual amount of gold, for which service you will be charged storage and insurance fees. An *unallocated* account will give you title to a specified amount of gold which is part of a pool held by the broker. This attracts lower holding charges, as the amount actually held by the broker is less than the combined allocation of his clients, in much the same way that a bank holds only a small proportion of the cash owned by its customers.

An unallocated account can also be used for trading. If you have a good credit reference, your broker may allow you to purchase gold on margin – which is to say that you pay only a proportion of the cost of the gold you acquire. You borrow the rest from the broker. If you are sure that the price is due to rise, and wish to speculate, then a trading account will allow you to do so and take quick profits. However, if you are wrong and the price falls, you may have to sell at a loss and end up owing your broker money.

For example, suppose you buy 10 ounces of gold at $300 an ounce, for a total price of $3,000. You pay the broker only 50 per cent of this, borrowing the rest. The price to you is only $1,500. Following a financial panic caused by the threat of war in the Middle East, you then sell the gold for $450 an ounce, making $4,500 in total. Your profit is $1,500 ($4,500 minus $3,000), which is 100 per cent of your original investment. But if you had bought the gold you could afford ($1,500 worth), your profit would be only $750, or 50 per cent. Leverage has doubled your gains.

Of course, if the price fell to, say, $200 an ounce, you would owe your broker $500 in addition to your own loss of $500. So you would have to be very convinced that the risk was worth it. An added complication is the foreign currency risk when you trade in dollars. If the pound falls relative to the dollar at the same time the gold price rises, your profits will be hit.

Other Precious Metals

Other metals of interest to the investor are silver, platinum and palladium. Silver and platinum are of course used for jewellery as well as for industrial purposes. Palladium is used only by industry, notably in the catalytic convertors which reduce exhaust pollution in motor vehicles.

The markets for all precious metals are volatile, and world industrial and financial trends have to be monitored carefully if you are to profit from these. This means that the precious metals speculator needs to find out a great deal about the subject before putting any cash on the line.

In the past, investors used to watch carefully the ratio of the price of one precious metal in relation to another. For example, for a long period gold used to fluctuate within fairly narrow boundaries of 10 to 15 times the price of silver. However, that ratio has crashed at certain points to as much as 100:1. This has led traders to doubt the validity of ratio analysis. But it remains a tool of investment appraisal. And silver did recover sharply from this historic low point against gold, which it sank to in March 1991.

Futures Trading

Probably the most exciting, and certainly the most hazardous form of speculation is futures trading in commodities and financial markets. We have already seen how it is possible to buy gold and other precious metals on margin, to amplify the possible gains. You can do this for over 50 commodities and markets. Some people even make a living out of it! One of the more famous American traders makes millions every year, having started with only $30,000. But he does admit to having to change his shirt four times a day!

Commodities markets are divided into 'metals' , such as copper, zinc and aluminium, and 'soft commodities', such as cocoa, rubber and oil. Financial futures markets are also made for currencies and bonds, and for stock indices such as the FTSE (Financial Times Stock Exchange), or 'Footsie' 100 share index. In each case the speculator buys and sells contracts made up of notional bundles of the goods or financial instruments. The contracts are for delivery in the future, and the speculator hopes to profit from rapid changes in the prices of the contracts before they fall due.

To take a simple example, a speculator might buy a contract for 100 tons of cocoa, due for delivery in December, which is three months hence. He or she expects the price to rise. This is known as 'going long' on cocoa. If the price rises over the next couple of weeks or so, the contract can be sold for a quick profit. If this is done on margin, the profit will be that much greater.

If the trader expects the price of cocoa to fall, then he or she will 'sell short'. That is to say, sell a contract now which he or she does not yet actually own, hoping to buy it later (that is, when it is due for delivery) at a lower price. This is a very hazardous way of making profits, because if the trader is wrong and the price of the contract rises, he or she will be forced to pay a much-inflated price in order to cover the contract. If the deal has been done on margin, the losses will be that much greater.

Only about 10 per cent of commodities traders are reckoned to make money consistently at the game, which rules it out for the average investor who wants to hold onto his or her capital and see it grow. It is possible to opt for a discretionary account, where you hand over your hard-earned cash to a professional broker to manage on your behalf. But these accounts are just as prone to wipe-outs. This is why it is useful to know about futures trading, but not necessarily to practise it!

Financial Bookmaking

It is possible to place a bet on the markets in much the same way as you might bet on a horse race. A financial bookmaker will allow you to bet on the direction of a variety of stock-market indices and the prices of commodities and currencies. In common with conventional brokers, the punter will be quoted a spread of buying and selling prices. For example, you might be quoted 2150–2160 for the Footsie 100 index. If you expect the index to rise, you place an 'up bet', putting down stake money as agreed with the bookmaker. This is to cover you if the bet goes against you, at which point you will owe the bookmaker money. For every point that the Footsie rises above 2160 over the period of the bet you will receive £10. Conversely, if you believe that the index will fall, you would place a 'down bet', and would receive £10 for every point that the index falls below 2150.

Unlike conventional betting, if you are wrong and the market goes against you, you may lose *more* than your stake money, which makes betting on the financial markets similarly risky to futures trading. If you had bet £500 on margin, and the index moved more than 50 points away from the offer price, then you would be required to put up more margin to stay in the bet. If you did not do this, the bookmaker would automatically close out your position and demand any balance owing. Alternatively, you could establish an automatic stop-loss limit (which you can also do with a futures trade) by instructing the bookmaker to sell if the market falls or rises beyond a set point. In this way you could be sure of minimizing your losses – unless the market was moving so fast that the bookmaker could not execute the order in time.

Fans of financial betting point out that unlike conventional trading, all of your gains are tax free, so you do not have to worry about possible capital gains liabilities. The possibility of stop-loss trading is also attractive. But there is always the potential for losing more than your stake money.

Traded Options

If you want to bet on the markets in a relatively painless way, then you might consider traded options. With this form of speculation you can at least limit your losses to the price of the option, as you will not be trading on margin. The worst that can happen is that the market moves against you and you lose some or all of the money you paid for the option, plus the broker's fee. But you cannot lose more than this.

An option is simply the right to buy or sell a share, or a given level of a stock index, at a given price. Options are divided into the conventional type, which you simply buy and hold for the life of a share, and traded options, which you can sell as well as buy. You can also *exercise* a traded option, that is, convert it into shares – or in the case of the Footsie index, cash, which is paid out by the Stock Exchange at £10 per index point.

Some 60 shares, as well as the Footsie itself, are traded daily. You will find the prices of put options and call options for various months listed in the newspaper. A *call option* is the right to buy a share at a given price; a *put option* is the right to sell at a given price. Prices are given in pence, but the minimum amount you can buy is a contract of 1,000 options. So an option priced at 10 pence will cost £100 per contract.

Suppose that in January you believe that the price of ICI shares is set to rise sharply, perhaps because you have a feeling that the company is about to announce record interim profits. The share price is currently 810 pence, so you buy a March call option at 30 pence per share exercisable at 850 pence, that is, you are paying

30 pence per share for the right to buy ICI shares at 850 pence per share. The option will rise in value if the share price rises above 850 at any time between now and 31st March. If it does so you will be able to sell your option at a profit.

The option has time value attached to it, which means that it will be more expensive the longer the time span between when you buy it and its date of expiry. It may also have intrinsic value if it is 'in the money'. This means that if you buy a February call option exercisable at 810 pence and the shares are already trading at 820 pence, 10 pence of the price of the option will represent its intrinsic value. The remainder of the price of the option will represent its time value. Thus, if the February 810 option costs 50 pence, then 10 pence is intrinsic value and 40 pence time value. Brokers will attempt to calculate what prices represent fair value, and those options that are under- or overpriced.

You can make a lot of money on options if you get your timing right. Put options on the Footsie went up to 5 or 6 times their previous value following the dramatic crash of October 1987, and again in July 1990 following the Iraqi invasion of Kuwait. Some people use charts based on theories such as the Elliot wave principle to decide when to buy and sell, while others rely on their own intuition and judgement. Risks can be spread through the operation of 'straddles' – simultaneous purchasing of put and call options to exploit rapid and contrary moves in prices.

Options are also a useful way for shareholders to hedge against risk. They can buy put options on the shares they are holding in order to protect themselves against falling share prices. They will also be able to get extra income from writing options – that is to say, by agreeing to sell their shares at given prices. If the option is not exercised, the writer pockets the premium paid by the buyer of the option. As most options are not exercised, but traded until expiry, this can be a painless way of accumulating extra cash from a portfolio of blue-chip shares.

Dealing in Options

If you are tempted to deal in traded options, or indeed in any other kind of speculation, it is important that you choose a reputable broker who is registered with the AFBD – the Association of Futures Brokers and Dealers (see the Appendix for the address). An up-to-date list of registered brokers is available from the Stock Exchange. It is not a good idea to be tempted by some of the unregistered operators who may cold-call you or offer you inducements to set up immediate accounts. A registered broker will in any case take pains to ensure that you are capable of meeting your financial obligations, and it will take two or three weeks to take up references before an account is opened.

It is important to avoid unlicensed brokers because they are always in danger of going under and taking your profits with them. Futures and options trading is not for the faint-hearted, nor for the financially insecure. Choose the right broker to get off to a good start. As the risk of loss is high, it is pointless to trade with money that you cannot afford to lose. It is likely that you will already have put away a fair amount in cash, bonds or blue-chip shares beforehand. Your gambling money is that which you are fully prepared to lose – without losing any sleep over it!

Also, it is obviously not a good idea to risk your whole stake on one or two trades. It would be better to divide the available capital into several slices – preferably 10. That way you are more likely to stay in the game. The best value is to generally to be found in options which are 'out of the money', which is to say that they are outside the exercise price. When buying these options, you are hoping that the index will move quickly to put them in the money and make them shoot up in value. But even out-of-the-money contracts can be expensive. An average contract on the Footsie 100 index is going to cost from £500 to £1,000, although short-term contracts bought on shares can be much cheaper, at £100 to £200.

It is best to practise trading on paper first, with an imaginary set of contracts. That way you will get used to interpreting the price charts and will learn to pay attention to the often rapid daily gyrations of share prices and the Footsie Index. Options trading is not something you can pick up and drop – when you are trading you will need to be in daily contact with the market and have unlimited access to your broker.

Getting it right and seeing your money double in a few days is a great feeling! And remember you can always cut your losses if things go wrong by selling on the option. So by all means have a go if you can afford to do so and if you have the right temperament.

Warrants

These are well suited to people who prefer to take a long view of a market. They are essentially long-term options, giving you the right to buy and sell shares, currencies and stock indices up to several years in the future (whereas traded options operate only for a maximum of six months or so).

Warrants are issued by companies and are traded in much the same way as options, by the same type of brokers, so you should be able to open an account dealing in both options and warrants. They are available for company shares, and large companies also issue warrants for currencies and stock indices. For example, you might buy a FTSE put warrant issued by British Telecom allowing you to exercise at a level of 2,300 or below. The lower the level of the index in the future, the more money you will make, either by exercising the warrant or by selling it at a profit.

The long period over which the warrant is operational makes this a more leisurely and less frantic decision-making process than is the case with options. For this reason they may be preferred by armchair speculators who want to be able to sleep well at night.

Other Forms of Speculation

There are lots of ways of speculating, in the sense of buying things which you expect will increase dramatically in value, such as land, property, and collector's items such as antique furniture, paintings, stamps, coins, classic cars, and so on. If you are keen on collecting a certain category of items because they give you pleasure for their own sake, regardless of their current market price, then by all means do so. If on the other hand you are thinking of collecting only for profit, then this strategy does *not* recommend itself in the economic conditions which currently apply and which are likely to exist well into the next century.

We are in a period of global deflation and falling asset values. This has already made its presence felt cruelly in markets such as land, property, and collector's items of all kinds. Such 'investments' will not be worthy of the name until we are at the bottom of the long-wave cycle, and even then investors will have a long wait before they see the kind of appreciation witnessed in the inflationary 1970s and the exceptional boom conditions of the 1980s.

For this reason you would be better to limit speculation to financial markets in which you are willing to gain expertise, or to those markets where you can already claim enough knowledge to recognize a bargain when you see one. There is of course no requirement that you should speculate at all in order to build wealth – compound interest allied to a careful investment programme will ensure that anyway. Speculation satisfies the gambling instinct which most of us seem to have to a greater or lesser degree. But it must be controlled, and used to add spice to life – not to ruin it!

Key Points

- Speculation can add good profits to your portfolio – as long as you take the time to learn about and then practise your chosen methods. It is generally a form of gambling, rather than investment.

- Gold can play a special role, as a hedge against economic disaster. It can also be used for short-term speculative trading.

- Futures trading can be immensely lucrative, but can also lead to losses in excess of the money originally gambled. This is not a game for the amateur investor.

- Options and warrants are more suited to the amateur, as the downside risk is limited and the potential profits large. But they are still not to everybody's taste.

- Understand the risks and try to limit them if you want to speculate. Only use money that you can afford to lose. Enjoy the game and you will probably be successful.

CHAPTER 12

Minimizing Your Tax Bill

Personal taxes have been cut in recent years from the high levels they reached in the 1970s, but they remain the largest single source of expenditure for many households (with the possible exception of mortgage payments). And, unlike mortgages, they are with you throughout your life, whether you are working or retired.

The money you earn as your salary might make you feel quite well off, but it is your *gross* earnings. The money you keep *after* tax is the important measure of your economic well-being. If you have been over-paying tax in the past, then an adjustment to your present tax-code and a refund from the taxman will be as good as a pay rise!

Unless you are self-employed, you will not automatically get an annual tax return. You may have to ask for one to ensure that your coding is correct. An important part of your wealth-creation strategy will be to request an annual return, so you can make sure that you are receiving all the allowances due to you and that you do not unintentionally evade any tax on investments due to the Inland Revenue. The penalties for tax evasion include fines and interest on the money owing.

On the other hand, it is perfectly legitimate to practise tax *avoidance*, whereby you seek to minimize your personal taxes. This is the duty of every serious investor. It should be approached with a little extra effort, just as you would employ in selecting a successful investment. The effort will pay off handsomely.

Personal Allowances

Everyone is entitled to a personal tax allowance. The figures are changed every year to allow for inflation and the policies of the government of the day. The current personal allowance for the 1991/92 tax year is £3,295. In addition to this there is an allowance for married couples, which can either be added to the allowance of the main earner or divided equally between the two partners. The current married couple's allowance is £1,720 in addition to the personal allowance quoted above.

There are two separate tax bands that are applied to taxable income, that is income *after* any allowances have been deducted. The first band is 25 per cent, and is for people whose *taxable* incomes are up to £23,700 a year. In other words, if you are single you can earn up to £26,995 before you move into the higher tax band. Everything you earn over this level is taxed at the higher rate of 40 per cent.

Your personal tax allowance is defined in your tax code, which will appear on your pay slip. The code has a letter, denoting your tax status (single, married, etc.), and a three-digit figure, which denotes your allowances. For example, 329L would mean that you were single and receiving only the basic allowance. Additional allowances might be made for other expenditures, such as for a personal pension.

While personal tax rates have been cut and the tax bands simplified under the Conservative Government, there is no guarantee that tax rates will not increase again under the pressures of higher public spending requirements or through policy changes instituted by a new administration. Indeed, as the worldwide economic slump intensifies during the 1990s we should expect tax rates to increase as the burden of public spending rises, which is all the more reason why you should take advantage of available tax concessions and consider carefully your tax position when undertaking any investment.

Direct personal taxes are only a minor part of the taxes we pay. The majority derives from the 17.5 per cent levy of Value Added Tax (VAT) paid on the goods and services we buy. If the Government simultaneously cuts personal taxation and raises VAT, then its citizens may in fact be worse off in terms of spending power, although they might perceive themselves to be better off. The burden of taxation through indirect means is also indiscriminate – everyone pays the same regardless of their income. But there is little one can do to avoid it – except reduce consumption!

Capital Gains Tax

In addition to personal allowances, there is another basic allowance which is of great importance to the investor. You can make up to £5,500 each year in tax-free capital gains on investments sold in that tax year. If these investments have been bought in previous years, you are allowed to offset the effects of inflation on your gains. This makes it unlikely that the novice investor will exceed the Capital

Gains Tax (CGT) threshold for some years, adding powerfully to the effect of compound interest on making your investments grow.

The CGT allowance applies equally for wife and husband, giving a total household exemption of £11,000. However, it applies only to the investments held in each partner's name. So if you are in danger of exceeding the CGT allowance, you might consider transferring some of your assets to your spouse.

Tax Relief on Mortgages

Another important tax allowance is relief on the interest paid on mortgages. This applies only to the first £30,000 of the mortgage, a limit which has remained unaltered for many years and which has taken no account of changes in the general level of house prices. It is nevertheless an important concession, taking around £930 off the annual mortgage bill for each household at current interest rates.

Mortgage tax relief is deducted automatically at source by the payer under the MIRAS (which stands for 'Mortgage Interest Relief at Source') scheme. The relief applies only to the basic tax rate. Again, there is no guarantee that mortgage interest relief will continue indefinitely. The ability of two or more people to club together to purchase a house has already been terminated by restricting MIRAS to one per household. If the relief is completely abolished in the future, it should have a deflationary effect on house prices, as people will be unable to borrow as much as they could previously.

Holiday Homes

A useful inducement for people who are thinking of investing some spare cash in a holiday home is tax relief on interest paid for the mortgage, provided that the home is used for holiday lets. It must be available for letting for more than 140 days a year, of which 70 days must attract lettings. The longest letting period allowable for any one tenant is one month.

The attractiveness of a holiday home for lettings would depend upon its location and consequent letting potential; and the purchase price in relation to its likely income. If a cottage or flat is purchased at the top of the economic cycle, when property is expensive, then it is unlikely to be a good investment. If purchased at the bottom of the cycle, when a good rate of return can be expected, then there is the prospect of capital growth on the property as well as income from lettings.

Capital growth will be subject to capital gains tax, if this is in excess of your personal allowance, but may still be spectacular over the long haul. If a holiday letting property is held until you retire, then under current legislation capital gains tax will not be payable if you sell it after retirement, subject to a maximum threshold of £150,000.

The potential yield on a letting property will need to be calculated net of running costs, which could be quite high. These would include letting and management fees to an agency, if you were unable to undertake these tasks yourself, property tax and property maintenance. These charges will take at least 20 per cent off the letting income. Balanced against this would be savings made on family holiday accommodation, provided that you did not object to visiting the same place every year!

Tax Relief on Pensions

The importance of taking advantage of the tax concessions available to those willing to take out a personal pension, or to top up their existing pension through additional voluntary contributions, has already been discussed in chapter 8. The relief is available up to different thresholds depending upon your age group, but the limits are generous.

Tax relief at the basic rate for a personal pension is normally claimed by the company on your behalf, so the amount deducted from your pay should be net of tax. If you are a higher-rate taxpayer you will need to have your tax code adjusted to take account of the extra allowance. Write to the Inland Revenue if you are in this position.

Company Cars

Over half of the new cars sold each year are owned by companies. Many of these are driven by individuals for both business and personal use. The use of a company car is often offered to executives as an important fringe-benefit attached to a job.

The use of a company car attracts extra personal taxation. The amount of additional tax you will have to pay will depend upon the how much mileage is used for personal purposes and the engine size of the car. As long as you drive the car in excess of 2,500 miles a year on company business, you will be taxed at the lower rate for each category of car.

For example, if you drive a 1.6-litre company car for which all the petrol bills are paid by the company, you will be taxed as if the benefit were equivalent to an extra £3,360 in salary. For a basic rate taxpayer this would mean an extra tax bill of £840 a year. This compares with the estimated £4,300 a year it would actually cost to buy and run a new car of the same type. So, despite the extra tax bill, a company car is still quite a perk!

The need for the Government to raise new revenues to match increased spending, coupled with public demands for less environmental pollution, means that the company car tax perk is increasingly under threat. A persistent erosion, if not the eventual abolition of tax relief on company cars can therefore be expected in the future.

Business Expansion Schemes

Wealthier investors might like to consider investing in a BES scheme. These schemes are designed to attract cash to risky new ventures whose shares are not listed on the stock-exchange. Up to £40,000 a year can be invested in BES schemes. Provided they survive, shares in the schemes can be sold free of capital gains tax. The investment must be for at least five years. Obviously you would want to be sure that the schemes in which you are investing are reasonably safe, and have good growth prospects.

Some of the most popular BES schemes have been those designed around the construction or purchase of residential property for lettings. Under assured tenancy schemes, landlords are protected from potential defaulters. During the property boom of the 1980s, BES residential property schemes grew in popularity as property values rocketed. Since the slump, existing investors have seen the value of their portfolios fall. But this state of affairs has produced opportunities for so-called 'vulture funds'. These BES schemes snap up unsold properties from distressed vendors at low prices. Sometimes whole developments will be purchased from property companies. Buying property in this manner gives purchasers a head start in ensuring that the BES fund will be profitable.

Enterprise Zone Trusts

There are 26 enterprise zones scattered throughout Britain, in which new businesses are encouraged to start up with a package of incentives, including exemptions from rates, 100 per cent capital allowances on commercial buildings, and simplified planning controls and regulations. So an investor can immediately write off tax against the cost of building commercial property in an enterprise zone.

Individuals can invest sums of £2,000 or so in trusts which have been set up especially to undertake property investment and management in enterprise zones. These trusts will charge joining fees and an annual management charge, just like a normal unit trust. Charges and performance will vary, so as usual it is worth shopping around.

In common with other types of property, if you undertake an investment of this type you will want to do so at the bottom of the economic cycle, when property has fallen from its inflationary peaks and once again offers good yields, and therefore good potential for capital appreciation. The 1990s are likely to be a classic period for this type of investment, so it is worth bearing it in mind for the long term, provided that you have the spare cash to invest at the right time.

Covenants

Turning from personal gain to charity, it is possible to give to your favourite causes in a cost-effective way by completing a deed of covenant. This allows the charity to reclaim 25 per cent of the amount you give. If you are a higher-rate taxpayer you can claim an additional 15 per cent back for yourself. Contact your favourite charities for the necessary forms, which are simple to complete.

Another form of giving, on the same tax-free basis, is through deductions at source from your monthly payroll. The taxman allows you to donate up to £600 a year in this way. Your employer should be able to make the necessary arrangements.

Inheritance Taxes

It may not be very pleasant to think about inheritance taxes, but provided that you have started your personal investment programme early enough, you will almost certainly exceed the taxable limits for inheritance, currently set at £140,000. The tax rate applied to estates above this limit is 40 per cent. Many people with a house fully paid for will already be close to the threshold. So if you want your nearest and dearest or your favourite charities to benefit as much as possible, you will need to give inheritance tax some thought, particularly as you approach retirement.

Another important point, which is ignored by all too many people, is the necessity of making a will. If you die without having done so, in a situation which is described by legal language as 'intestate', then your assets will be disposed of according to strict priorities established by the State. If you are married, the first £75,000 will pass to your spouse; the remainder will be divided equally between your spouse and your children. If you are married with no children, your spouse receives up to £125,000, with the remainder divided between your spouse and your parents. If your parents are not alive your brothers and sisters will be entitled to your parents' share.

There are further rules for dividing the estates of deceased people with no spouses or children, and for unmarried parents. So if you are unhappy at the possibility of your estate passing to

people other than those you want to protect to the fullest, then you will need to have a will drawn up by a solicitor. This is not expensive, and will safeguard your loved ones. You will also need to appoint an executor – someone who will ensure that your will is properly carried out after your death.

Apart from the relatively simple procedure of drawing up a will, inheritance tax planning is really a specialized subject, and can become complicated. Those with large estates will require the services of experts. Even so, the basic concepts are straightforward. Essentially you can dispose of assets in excess of the taxable limit (currently £140,000) in two ways. The first is by means of gifts. Provided that you survive for seven years after the gift has been made, then it will not be taxed. However, once it has been made you cannot reclaim the gift as a way of avoiding tax.

The second method is to set up a trust, which is designed to dispose of your assets to the desired beneficiaries without attracting tax. A trust is simply a device by which you relinquish control of your assets to a board of 'trustees' who are strictly bound to dispose of those assets according to the rules of the particular kind of trust which has been established.

Making Gifts

Gifts can be made to your spouse, free of tax, at any time and of any amount. Both spouses are further allowed to give up to £3,000 each year free of tax to other beneficiaries, and one year's annual exemption can be carried forward into the next. If you start early enough, a series of annual exemptions can quickly reduce the balance of your assets. Gifts of this type can be made to individuals and to accumulation and maintenance trusts where named individuals, such as your children, will benefit.

If you wish to make gifts in excess of this limit, this can be done with 'potentially exempt transfers' (PETs). These require you to stay alive for seven years after the gift has been made – which is why they are considered only *potentially* exempt. If you die during this period, the recipient will be liable to tax on a sliding scale based on the death rate of 40 per cent. The scale rates are given in Table 14.

PETs are an important exemption for people with estates that exceed the tax-free limit, so transfers will have to take place well in advance of your anticipated death if you wish your beneficiaries to gain the full advantage. Of course, no one knows when they will die, so if you need to transfer your assets do so earlier rather than later. Also, the definition of gifts can get complicated, which is why you may need to consult a professional tax adviser. If you do it yourself,

Table 14: Sliding Scale of Death Tax Rate

Years between gift and death	Tax rate on the gift
0–3	40%
3–4	32%
4–5	24%
5–6	16%
6–7	8%
more than 7 years	nil

be sure that the dates and amounts of the transfer are recorded and left with your executor.

Establishing a Trust

A trust can be created either during the lifetime of the settlor (the person leaving the inheritance) or provided for by the settlor's will. It is advantageous to set up a trust during your lifetime, as the PET rules will then apply. Otherwise trusts set up after your death will be treated as inheritances, and may thus be liable to tax.

There are three main types of trust:

1. interest in possession;
2. accumulation and maintenance; and
3. discretionary.

Interest in Possession Trusts

Interest in possession trusts allow the beneficiaries an income for life, which is why they are known as 'life tenants' of the trust. The beneficiaries' inheritors in turn are entitled to the capital. This type of trust is often used as a marriage settlement, allowing the wife to retain an income independently of her husband and to pass the capital on to her children, for example. Income tax will be payable at normal rates on income derived from the trust.

Accumulation and Maintenance Trusts

Accumulation and maintenance trusts are used for children or youths who may not be considered old enough to manage their own incomes. They allow the trustees to dispose of the income for the benefit of the child (for example in payment of school fees) or to retain and add it to the capital until the beneficiary reaches the age of 25. After that the income is paid directly to the beneficiary, but the trustees can retain control of the capital if they see fit. Income tax is payable by the trustees or by the beneficiary when he or she takes control of the income.

Discretionary trusts

Discretionary trusts allow the trustees to decide who should be the beneficiaries, subject only to legal restrictions on the type of beneficiary. These might include spouses, children or grandchildren, their relatives by marriage, or charities. Capital or income can be distributed, as the trustees deem appropriate. Discretionary trusts may be used to benefit a surviving spouse while keeping the capital out of his or her estate. Inheritance tax is payable on this type of trust, whether or not it is set up in the lifetime of the benefactor.

Capital gains taxes are payable on discretionary trusts at the rate of 30 per cent, with the annual exemption being half that of the normal individual rate (i.e. £2,750).

The facts set out here about inheritance tax are necessarily brief, but should provide you with enough information to make a decision as to whether inheritance tax planning is going to be necessary. If it is, then you will need to contact a specialist, as this branch of taxation can soon become complicated. Further information is also available from the specialist tax guides listed in the Appendix.

Key Points

- The money you earn is what you keep after tax, not your gross salary. Tax will quite probably be your greatest single lifetime expenditure.

- Taxation might seem to be a dry subject, but it is worth grasping the basics to save yourself money. Tax saved or reclaimed is as good as a pay rise.

- It is important to complete a tax declaration form each year in order to keep abreast of your entitlements and liabilities. You may have to ask for one.

- The £5,500 capital gains tax allowance will be a major boost to your investment programme.

- Always consider the tax position of an investment, but don't invest only for tax breaks. Business expansion schemes and enterprise zone trusts may seem attractive, but they do have risks attached.

- Make out a will and plan your inheritance strategy early if you want your loved ones to benefit to the maximum. Get professional advice if your estate is larger than the tax-free minimum.

CHAPTER 13

Investing for Income

So far I have concentrated on ways in which you can convert your income into capital, building up a sizable portfolio over time. But there will inevitably be a time when you will need to convert your capital into income, such as when you stop work to start a family, or when you retire. In this chapter we'll take a look at which investments are likely to be appropriate when these circumstances arise.

Investing for income does not mean that capital growth should be sacrificed. Investments will need to grow by the rate of inflation in order to keep up their real value. If you are drawing a pension, for example, you would be wise to continue the savings habit and put a proportion of that income into growth investments, which can in turn boost the value of your income-generating portfolio in the future. It is also the case that many of the characteristics of good growth investments apply equally to income investments. If you put your money into cash holdings, you will still want the best interest rate you can get without sacrificing a reasonable degree of security. If you find a share with a high yield, it may be undervalued and offer good growth prospects as well.

Safety First

In my financial files I keep a memento. I acquired it by replying to an advertisement when I first became interested in investment in government bonds, not long before the great crash of October 1987. It is a glossy brochure from a firm promising capital growth with perfect safety through investment in gilts. Among other claims it says that it can offer 'absolute protection of your investment' because the investment is made in 'government securities which are widely recognized as one of the most secure types of investment'. The brochure goes on to state that all cash and securities are held in the name of a major British bank.

The pamphlet is glossy, the presentation reassuring. But the firm is Barlow Clowes, engineers of one of the most spectacular investment rip-offs of this century. Many of their victims were retired people who had sunk their life savings into the firm. They have had to wait years in the hope of compensation.

Barlow Clowes was licensed, although misgivings had been expressed by the statutory body dealing with the firm, and it continued to be promoted by financial intermediaries, the majority of whom were acting in good faith.

The Barlow Clowes example demonstrates forcefully the three rules of investing:

1.   As far as possible make your own arrangements by dealing directly with the investment institutions.
2.   Choose the biggest and most reputable institutions.
3.   Diversify to minimize risk.

The trade-off between the risks and rewards of investing has already been discussed in chapter 5. If an investment firm offers results in excess of the norm you should always be very suspicious. The income investor will need to put capital protection above all else, as capital may not be possible to rebuild once lost.

Your Tax Position

You will need to be clear at the outset about your tax position. Say, for example, that you are married and that you have no income other than that from your investments. If this income falls below your personal tax allowance (see chapter 12), then all of it will be tax-free. If necessary, you may need to transfer the married person's allowance from your spouse's income to your own in order to maximize the tax allowance. In this way you could earn up to £6,375 (depending upon your age) from your investments without being subjected to tax.

If your income does put you below the tax threshold, you will immediately be looking for investments which pay interest gross, that is, before taxes are deducted. Certain National Savings schemes, bank and building society accounts, and offshore funds pay interest gross. Some of these have already been discussed in chapter 6.

Savings Accounts

Banks and building societies offer certain accounts designed especially for non-taxpayers, which pay interest gross. Some accounts also offer to pay interest monthly, giving a steady flow of

income to those who require it. The best interest rates are offered
to people willing to lock their money up for longish periods ranging
from three months to a year. The interest rate also rises in line with
the amount deposited.

Offshore accounts automatically pay interest gross. Unfortunately, they offer no protection to the investor. You will also have to
declare interest on such accounts on your tax form, and pay tax on
them if necessary. In view of this potential risk to your funds, it is
best to choose one of the larger banks with which to hold an
offshore account. The interest rates can be very attractive, even
allowing for the extra risk.

National Savings offer an 'investment account' which is even
more secure than a bank or a building society, and which also
offers interest gross, paid at competitive rates. However, interest is
only paid on an annual basis. One month's notice is required for
withdrawals, and £5 is the minimum investment.

Many people are apparently content to put their money on
deposit and draw an income from it. Unfortunately, if they cream off
all the income, leaving none for capital growth, then the value of the
capital sum will swiftly be eroded by inflation. Table 15
demonstrates this.

Table 15: Effects of Inflation on £100,000 after 10 years

Inflation Rate	Real Value
5%	£61,391
7.5%	£48,519
10%	£38,554

It can be seen then that the important calculation that needs to be
made by the income investor is the *real* rate of interest. If you can
earn 10 per cent on your cash balance, and inflation is running at
5 per cent, then the real rate of interest is 5 per cent. In order to
maintain the value of the capital sum, you would have to reinvest
5 per cent of the income, leaving you 5 per cent to spend. If you
had originally calculated the capital sum required to produce an
appropriate amount of income for your needs, you would now have
to double it.

However, there is some good news for people who have already
paid off their mortgages. The inflation rate in the UK is calculated
according to different conventions than those of our European
Community partners. In recent years it has been overstated
through the inclusion of mortgage interest payments, and has not
included the effects of house prices. If these adjustments are made,
up to 2 per cent can be lopped off the index.

Each month the *Sunday Times* publishes an inflation index produced by the Institute of Fiscal Studies, which could be taken as the true measure of inflation, at least for the purposes of international comparisons. You may like to adopt this measure according to your own circumstances. Those readers with mortgages, however, may prefer to use the official version!

Of course, if you have a large capital sum and do not feel that you are likely to need to live off it for very long, you may feel it doesn't matter if it depreciates a bit. But this is an unnecessarily drastic course to take. It would be better to keep up the savings habit and maintain the value of your capital. There are also investments such as gilts and shares which under appropriate circumstances can grow in value while at the same time paying an income. These are discussed later in this chapter.

Income Bonds

Income bonds are issued by National Savings and by insurance companies. They are designed in a variety of ways to satisfy different requirements. The non-taxpayer will be interested in the National Savings version, which pays interest gross, on a monthly basis. The capital is of course guaranteed, and is repaid to you when you cash in the bond. Three months' notice is required, and the bonds should be held for at least a year. One drawback with income bonds is that the interest rate fluctuates in line with general market conditions, just as it does in a normal savings account.

Guaranteed income bonds are issued by insurance companies and are useful to the tax payer, because interest is paid net of tax. Interest payments are usually *fixed* for the life of the bond, which can be anything from one to ten years. This means that guaranteed income bonds are attractive during periods of high interest rates which can be expected to fall in the future.

The bonds take various forms, split into type A, B, C, D, etc. Their precise characteristics vary, but they follow two basic themes. You can purchase an endowment policy, or series of policies, which repay the capital on the bond; or you can purchase an annuity which also repays the capital.

Most common are type-B bonds, which are single premium endowment bonds incorporating a guaranteed rate of return. Up to 5 per cent of your investment can be deferred for the purposes of higher-rate tax until the end of the term of the bond. The advantage of this is that the bondholder could by then fall into a lower tax bracket, for example if he or she has retired. The way in which extra interest is calculated is also to the advantage of higher-rate taxpayers, who will pay less than they would if receiving the same rate of interest on conventional cash accounts.

Type-A and -C bonds are variations on the theme of purchasing annuities, which can provide streams of income to suit the purposes of the investor. These are not offered by many companies, but they have the advantage of allowing non-taxpayers to receive interest payments gross. Another variety of guaranteed income bond, known as type F, takes the form of a whole life policy, which pays an income for the life of the bondholder. This income is paid net of basic rate tax.

Guaranteed income bonds are complicated animals, and you will probably need the help of a company specialist or a good intermediary to select the type which is right for you. But the main advantage of locking into fixed interest rates when conditions are right applies to all of these types of investment.

Investment in Gilts

You will recall from chapter 9 that conventional Government bonds, known as gilt-edged securities, are exceptionally safe and offer both guaranteed levels of income and the prospect of capital gains. As such, they are of particular interest when conditions are right. If you are locked into high interest rates, and rates subsequently fall, the capital value of your gilt holdings will rise. This gives you that rare advantage, secure income with capital gains!

Income investors who are non-taxpayers, or who only pay basic rate tax, will be tempted to buy gilts offering higher rates of interest. If the investment is to be long term, then gilts offering long dates to maturity will be appropriate. Here the undated issues are also useful. They are perpetual gilts, with no expiry date, unless redeemed by the Government at face value, which is highly unlikely.

When interest rates fall, long-dated and undated gilts offer the greatest potential for capital gain, helping you to defy inflation. When you feel that interest rates have reached a low point, you can sell the gilts at a profit and invest the proceeds in some other form of income-earning security with potential for capital gain, such as high-yielding shares.

The shape of the gilt yield curve is of particular importance to income investors. If the curve takes a conventional shape, interest rates at the long end will be higher than short-term rates. However, if the reverse occurs, during the special periods associated with recessions, longer-term investors will be penalized by lower yields, despite the higher levels of risk which they are taking on. But inverted yield curves do not last for long, and equilibrium is eventually restored.

Convertibles

As interest rates fall, the value of your gilt holdings rises. But when interest rates are low, shares begin to look increasingly attractive. You can invest in ordinary shares (equities), but their yields might not be very attractive, and there is always risk attached, even for alpha stocks, and especially during a bear market. You might then be tempted to enter the market, but still desirous of a reasonable yield in excess of that produced by ordinary shares, and with more safety. If so, convertible stock may be what you are looking for.

Convertibles, as discussed in chapter 9, are loan stocks issued by companies which pay a coupon (fixed rate of interest) just like a normal bond or preference share. The income from the convertible is paid out twice a year. At certain dates during the life of the stock you are allowed to convert it into the company's ordinary shares. The terms of the conversion are set when you buy the stock, for example, for every 100 convertible stocks you hold you may be allowed to convert to 75 ordinary shares. Although the terms are not one-for-one, the dividend paid by the convertible will be higher than that paid by ordinary shares at the time of purchase, so you are getting extra income.

You will pay extra for the right to hold a convertible, the difference being expressed as a percentage, and called the premium. Premiums vary depending upon the terms of the convertible – and sometimes they can be bought at a discount. This usually happens when the price of the ordinary share moves up rapidly and the convertible takes time to readjust.

If you buy convertibles when their yields are attractive and when shares are moving up in a bull market, you can have the best of both worlds – steady income with capital growth. The long wave informs the income investor that the early to mid-1990s should be a good time to consider buying convertibles.

Convertibles can be bought through a broker. Your broker should be able to supply you with a list of convertibles, giving their price, conversion terms, yields and premiums as compared with ordinary shares. As with investment in ordinary shares, stick to alpha stocks, and seek out shares that have good prospects. If you invest just for high yield, you may be buying into a dud company. Remember the safety first rule for income investors.

High-yielding Ordinary Shares

Another way of getting income with the potential for capital growth is by purchasing high-yielding shares. These come from companies that have generally fallen out of popular favour, so their price is low relative to their earnings. A low price/earnings ratio is one indicator of share bargains, other things being equal.

The reason for the low price of shares such as these is the fear that the shares will not actually pay increasing dividends in the future. Of course this is a risk, especially if the stock-market is on the way down and we are entering a recession. However, we already know that the market tends to overdo both optimism and pessimism. At the time of writing, bank shares are out of favour, so this sector offers high yields.

You will recall from chapter 10 that it is only worth investing in blue-chip alpha shares, as well as in certain second-line issues (betas). The gammas should be avoided. This is especially true for high-yielding shares. It is in fact rather unlikely that alpha shares will fail to pay a dividend, although dividends may be cut. You will always need to study potential share investments very carefully.

The best time to invest in high-yielding blue-chip shares is in the middle of a slump. By then pessimism will be universal, and bargains will abound. You will again be able to have your cake and eat it. Buy gilts on the way into the slump, and benefit from the capital gain as interest rates fall in an attempt to stimulate the economy. Sell at a profit, and invest the proceeds in convertibles and quality high-yielding shares. Then watch your investments gain value sharply as the stock-market recovers.

Unit and Investment Trusts

A good way to invest in a diverse portfolio of quality shares is to do so through a unit or investment trust. The pros and cons of these are discussed in chapter 10. Here it is worth noting that there are sectors of trust investment specifically for income investors.

Unit trusts offer two sectors for income investors – UK equity income and international equity income. These are aimed deliberately at shares yielding well in excess of the average of the market as a whole. Investment trusts offer both of these sectors plus another entitled 'high income', which is a hybrid of the other two. Income can either be taken from the trusts or reinvested. In addition, the price of the units will grow if you have bought at the correct point along the market cycle.

It can of course be advantageous to buy into income-oriented unit and investment trusts through a Personal Equity Plan. You are allowed to invest up to half of your basic PEP allowance (currently £6,000 a year) in trusts. That way all your capital growth and income received will be tax free. Each PEP lasts a year, so you will get the income at the end of that period.

Annuities

Finally, you can always purchase an annuity. These are commonly bought with your pension fund when you realize the value of your investment. Annuities provide a stream of income for a specified period, or until you die.

You can buy annuities for various periods and offering different benefits. For example, you can choose a lower income which increases in line with inflation, or take a straight cash income which does not increase over the years. If you choose the latter your income will of course be steadily eroded in real terms.

The most competitive annuity rates currently offered are listed in professional money magazines. The best deals are for annuities which last until a person dies. For example, at current rates any of the top insurance companies will pay a man aged 60 around £1,500 a year for a £10,000 annuity. The rates payable to women at the retirement age of 60 are obviously lower, as statistically women live longer.

Short-term annuities are not good value in spite of the fact that they offer high interest rates. For example, you might be offered a 25 per cent interest rate over 5 years. But once you have purchased the annuity you have said goodbye to your capital. For this reason annuities are best purchased by retired people on a lifetime basis only.

Key Points

- The priority for income investors is security and preservation of their capital. Remember the Barlow Clowes fiasco.

- When real interest rates are high it can make good sense for income investors to keep their money in cash. However, a portion should be reinvested to reduce the effects of inflation.

- When interest rates are about to fall, income investors should lock into high rates by purchasing gilts and fixed-income insurance bonds, which offer a high level of security plus potential capital gain.

- When interest rates have bottomed out and the stock-market can be expected to rise, income investors should turn to convertibles and high-yielding alpha shares. These offer good yields and also the prospects of capital gain as the price of ordinary shares rises.

- Unit or investment trusts offer funds for income investors. Capital gains and income will be tax free if purchased through a PEP.

- Buy annuities to last from retirement until death. Temporary annuities are not good value, as you must kiss goodbye to your capital.

CHAPTER 14

Ensuring Your Prosperous Future

The last 40 years or so have been tremendously successful for investors. But the 1990s have already seen the investment climate changing, so it is important that we get an idea of the likely economic developments and how these might affect your savings and investment strategy.

Investment decisions can of course be made by you alone, without recourse to professionals. Often you can deal directly with the companies offering unit and investment trusts, pensions, and so on. Sometimes, however, you will need the advice of intermediaries, or will have no choice but to use the services of a stockbroker in order to make certain investments.

Wealth Creation

As long as you treat your savings plan as a personal tax which must be paid come what may, you will succeed in increasing your wealth. The power of compound interest will ensure that your savings multiply at an accelerating rate. For this reason alone, the sooner you start, the richer you will get. There is no time to put off planning your own financial prosperity. Begin by discovering where you are, and where you want to go. A savings programme will help you get there, but it will help you in more ways than just financially. Money in the bank builds your confidence. A plan helps you to get more out of life, instead of just drifting along. As you gain more skill at saving and investing, you will find yourself strengthening your career aims, improving your family life and relationships with friends, and enjoying your free time more. With direction, you have purpose, and with this success is guaranteed.

Using Financial Advisers

It may come as a surprise to you, but just by having read and absorbed the contents of this book you are already much better informed than are many of the 'professionals' in the money business. This includes financial advisers, stockbrokers, and bank managers. In fact, as you get more knowledgeable you will probably find yourself advising your advisers on certain aspects of investment!

Advisers should be used for specialist advice and information that you cannot get yourself. Inheritance planning, for example, is a complex and specialized subject. Remember, however, that an expert on inheritance planning is unlikely to know very much about share selection. Similarly, the financial advisers you see advertising in the local paper are basically salespeople for various financial schemes, which even they refer to as 'products'. Most of them operate wholly or partly on commission, and therefore have a vested interest in selling high-commission products.

To take but one example, <u>investment trusts</u> pay little or no commission, and are thus not sold in great quantities by financial intermediaries, who are more likely to promote higher-commission unit trusts. Financial advisers often have only a sketchy knowledge of the products they are selling. Try asking one of these salespeople about the precise performance of the unit trusts they are promoting. If my experience is anything to go by, few will be able to give you detailed replies.

It is also sad to see that so many employees of building societies, estate agents and the like are tied to one company's financial products. Although they are required by law to state this to their clients, many customers will automatically assume that their friendly local building society, bank or estate agency is going to give them the best deal, or at least will be as good as any other. We have seen, however, that investment performance can very a lot. It is especially sad to observe how salespeople will try to persuade their customers to take out endowment mortgages because these pay them a commission, when repayment mortgages might be more suitable.

You may need to consult financial intermediaries to get quotations for such things as life assurance policies, income bonds and mortgages. There is no harm in shopping around for the best deal. And you shouldn't be afraid to ask about commissions if you feel it is relevant to do so. A competent adviser will not take it amiss. Some advisers now offer a fee-only service, whereby you pay them up front and this is the only fee they get for their services, in which case you can perhaps be more sure of getting impartial advice.

A vital point to remember when dealing with financial advisers is that they should be fully accredited members of a statutory organization under the authority of the Securities and Investments Board, such as FIMBRA – the Financial Intermediaries, Managers and Brokers Regulatory Association – or LAUTRO – the Life Assurance and Unit Trust Regulatory Organisation (see the Appendix for addresses). As such they are licensed and your money is protected by the Security and Investments Board, the money industry's watch-dog.

Using a Broker

Some of the investments described in this book require that you use a stockbroker. Choose only firms that are members of the Stock Exchange. If you are dealing in options or futures, the firm should also be registered with AFBD, the Association of Futures Brokers and Dealers (see the Appendix for the address).

It is possible to buy and sell shares through banks as well as through brokers. The cheapest method is to use a 'no-frills', *execution-only* service, where you make the decisions and the brokers execute them. The next cheapest is an *advisory* service, where the brokers inform you of their analysts' recommendations and send you regular information bulletins concerning the state of the market and of the major shares. The most expensive method is the *discretionary* service, suitable only for clients with large amounts to invest. Here the brokers make all the buying and selling decisions, and charge you an annual management fee.

There is no reason why with a bit of thought and study you should not do as least as well as the professionals. After all, if they really understood the markets they would be very wealthy, and would not need to be full-time stockbrokers! Much of the gains that are made as a result of their advice will simply reflect general gains in the market. This is why it is so important to pay attention to the overall investment climate, and the point at which you are investing on the long wave.

The Importance of the Long Wave

We have dwelt at some length on the structure and interpretation of the long economic wave named after its discoverer, Nikolai Kondratieff. There are of course other waves, some much shorter that the Kondratieff wave, some even longer. But the Kondratieff wave is the most important one of all to the investor. In an otherwise bewildering world it explains with clarity and simplicity what exactly is happening to the economy, and why.

Do not be misled by the simplicity of the wave. The truth is not usually complex. The nature of the long wave explains the experience of the 1980s very well indeed. Having understand the nature of the secondary prosperity, it is but a short step to comprehending the implications for the 1990s. I am not suggesting that history repeats itself exactly, or that an understanding of the long wave gives you perfect clairvoyance, but it should help guide you into the correct long-term investment decisions. Remember, 'In the land of the blind, the one-eyed man is king'!

The investment world is full of people who assume that just because the last 10 or 20 years were good for certain types of investment, that the next couple of decades will be exactly the same. Many financial advisers believe this. But the future is not a straight-line progression from the past. During the 1970s there were lots of doom-and-gloom scenarios describing the imminent threat of the world running out of resources. During the 1980s, in a world of commodity gluts, such notions appeared ludicrous. Similarly, in the late 1980s employers were worried about the 'demographic time bomb', and wondered where they would find enough young people to fill the available jobs. In spite of this, you can be sure that during the 1990s youth unemployment will once again become a national problem.

Once a trend has become common knowledge, it will change. This is a part of mass psychology. The contrarian investor will always do well if he or she does the opposite of the herd, once the trend is mature enough.

Watch the Ratios

The long wave tells us basically which investments are likely to do well at each part of the cycle. Each of the three main investment categories – cash, bonds and shares – has its role to play. While many portfolios are likely to include all three types of investment, the weighting of each will change as conditions dictate. For example, you will be mainly in cash when the stock-market is in its final upward frenzy before the inevitable crash. You will move into bonds when real interest rates are high. You will buy shares and property when inflation begins to accelerate, and so on.

How do we know when to switch from one investment to another? We have two basic guides. One is our position on the long wave itself, which makes us ready for new trends and helps us to recognize them when they are underway. The other is an understanding of the key ratios applicable to each type of investment.

Thus, when rents are high relative to mortgage payments and real interest rates are low, you buy a house. When interest rates are high, you move into cash or bonds. When yields on shares are high and inflation is a worry, you buy shares. The more you invest, the more aware you will become of the relevant ratios. If the ratios tell you to sell – then sell! Warren Buffet, the famous US investor, sold nearly all his shares in 1986. He did this simply because the ratios he was using to define which shares to purchase did not show that there was any value left in the market. Shares were overvalued, so he sold up. Of course, the great crash subsequently proved him correct.

This is why I believe that investment is not difficult. What is most difficult is learning to follow your own instincts and careful analysis when all around you are doing the opposite! The frenzied bull markets in shares and property at the end of the 1980s produced a classic example of the bandwagon mentality that exists in most people. We shall not see the like again for at least 40 years. Our recent experience will be something to tell your grandchildren about (if you should have some!), and an example to give them warning of the results of folly. But your grandchildren will probably tell you that 'things are different now', just as in the 1980s many people thought the financial markets were different from those of the 1920s.

Investing in the 1990s

This is a fascinating period in which to begin a personal investment programme (or to write a book on the subject!). The global recession long predicted by followers of Kondratieff and so comprehensively pooh-poohed by vested interests is in full swing. As the slump deepens and lengthens, many people who have clung to their shares and houses hoping for an upturn will be disappointed. Some will dump their investments in despair, further depressing an already glutted market. This is where the new investor will benefit, purchasing assets for a fraction of their former value and holding them for the long bull markets to come.

This is why I am now optimistic and very cheerful, to the annoyance of those of my contemporaries who have invested in the wrong things at the wrong time. You do not have to repeat their mistakes, for you now understand the long wave and its significance. What a marvellous and exciting time to begin a programme of saving and investment!

As I write, the correct investment attitude is one of caution and patience. The astute investor is saving cash and locking it away in high-interest tax-free investments such as National Savings and TESSA accounts. Investors in bonds have already benefited from falling interest rates.

The bear market in shares is in full swing, but the stock-market is widely perceived by the majority of professionals (or at least those quoted by the mass media!) to represent good value, with P/E ratios as a whole at 13–14. But we have seen that in fact the market only represents good value when P/E ratios are under 10, and that is during bull phases (see Figure 4, page 94). In a severe bear market, P/E ratios will have to fall to at least 8 before they can be said to give good value. During the very severe crash of 1973 they fell below 6.

An interesting feature of this bear market is the way in which share values in the UK and USA have held up longer than one might expect, given the severity of the financial crisis, war in the Gulf, and the depth, breadth and strength of the global recession. It is often said that stock-markets anticipate events, falling well before a recession or rising well in advance of a recovery. The condition of the markets in early 1991 tells us that this is not always so. The markets will come down to earth rapidly and with a sharp bump, and will probably have done so by the time this book is published.

Japan's situation is of great interest. Unlike the UK and USA, the overvalued market there crashed to nearly half its previous value over the course of 1990. It has further to go, but will represent excellent value when the Nikkei index has gone down to around 10,000 from its peak of nearly 40,000. The coming century will be the Asian century, and investment in the stock-markets of the Pacific will bring the greatest rewards. You can participate in this success through unit trusts and investment trusts.

By 1992 or thereabouts the world's stock-markets should have completed their bear phase, and it will be time again to commit funds to the market. Your savings plan can then incorporate funnelling funds into appropriate investment trusts, perhaps through monthly savings schemes, or you might set up a PEP for your shareholdings. It will take courage to invest at this time, for the majority of investors will be very scared, having suffered devastating losses on their share portfolios and on property. But it will bring great rewards.

Interest rates should have fallen substantially by the mid-1990s, bringing lower returns for those investing in cash and bonds. These holdings will be liquidated progressively in favour of shares. As the world financial system continues to feel the strain of over-indebtedness, you may like to keep 5 per cent or so of your money in gold or gold shares, as a hedge against a collapse of confidence in the dollar, which until now has taken on the role of the world's reserve currency.

The dangers of financial collapse also mean that you must at this time (now and for the remainder of the 1990s) be extra specially careful to ensure the safety of your cash and bond investments. Choose only the largest banks and building societies. They may not pay the highest interest rates, but they will offer you the most safety.

Also be careful not to put all of your cash in one basket, or to exceed the limits at which the Government offers protection for accounts. Currently 75 per cent protection for the first £20,000 is offered by banks and 90 per cent by building societies.

The mid-1990s will be time once again to consider buying a house. By then prices should have fallen a long way from the peaks reached in the late 1980s. Mortgage funds will probably be harder to get, and you may need to save a substantial amount for the deposit. But the ratio of rents to prices will have risen, so it will make financial sense to be mortgaged once again. Prices will continue to fall if the slump is prolonged, but that should be of little concern to you if the decline has in most part already occurred.

Finally, do not neglect your pension and essential life assurance requirements. Retirement might seem to be a long way off, but one day it will come. By then you will be wealthy from your investment programme, and will be able to add a substantial income to your capital wealth. With careful management you will be able to pass on a substantial inheritance to your children. Your family will have broken out of the vicious cycle of poverty that entraps so many for so long.

The best investment you can make and the best inheritance you can leave is a knowledge of how to save and invest. Begin now to build wealth from your income, and enjoy the manifold benefits it brings.

Key Points

- Desire is more important than income in building wealth. The commitment to save will lead you to increase your income in many ways.

- You already know more than many experts. Use intermediaries and brokers only when you need to, otherwise trust your own judgement.

- Every investment has key ratios relevant to it which signal when to buy and when to sell. Observe and profit from them.

- An understanding of the economic long wave is critical to investment success. Mark your position on the wave and invest in accordance with it.

- The 1990s offer many opportunities to purchase financial assets at bargain prices. Seize these opportunities!

APPENDIX

Further Reading & Useful Addresses

Further Reading

General Reading

Beckman, Robert, *The Downwave: Surviving the Second Great Depression*, London: Pan, 1983.

- , *Into the Upwave*, Horndean: Milestone Publications, 1988.

Cobbett, Donald, *Money Trail, Money Trap: How to Win in the Stockmarket*, London: Mercury Business Books, 1989.

Davidson, James Dale, and Rees-Mogg, Sir William, *Blood in the Streets: Investment Profits in a World Gone Mad*, London: Sidgwick and Jackson, 1988.

Kirkland, D., and Kirkland, W., *Power Cycles*, Phoenix, Az: Professional Communications, 1985.

Kondratieff, Nicolai, 'The Long Wave of Economic Life', *Review of Economic Statistics*, 17, 6, November 1935.

Wood, Christopher, *Boom and Bust: The Rise and Fall of the World's Financial Markets*, London: Sidgwick and Jackson, 1988.

Personal Development

Cutler, Peter, *Get Out of Debt and Prosper*, London: Thorsons, 1990.

Fowler, Alan, and Fowler, Deborah, *Making Money Part Time*, London: Sphere Business Guidebooks, 1986.

Hill, Napoleon, *Think and Grow Rich*, Los Angeles: Wilshire Book Company, 1970 (distributed by Thorsons in the UK).

Lubbock, Bill, and Stokes, Richard, *How to Get a Job*, London: Hamlyn 'Help Yourself Guide', 1989.

Schwartz, D., *The Magic of Thinking Big*, Los Angeles: Wilshire Book Company, 1984.

Investment

Brett, Michael, *How to Read the Financial Pages*, London: Hutchinson Business Books, 1989.

Consumers' Association, *Which? Way to Save and Invest*, 2 Marylebone Road, London NW1 4DX, 1991.

The *Daily Mail*, *Money Mail Saver's Guide*, Harmsworth Publications Ltd., 1990.

Frost, A., and Prechter, Robert, *Elliot Wave Principle*, New Classics Library, 1985.

Goldstein-Jackson, Kevin, *Share Millions: How to Make Money on the Stock Market*, Tadworth: Paperfronts, 1989.

Tait, Nikki, *The Investors Chronicle Beginner's Guide to the Stockmarket*, Harmondsworth: Penguin, 1987.

Journals and Directories

Investors Chronicle (FT Business Information Ltd).

Money Managment (*Financial Times* Publications).

Money Observer (The *Observer*).

The Unit Trust Yearbook, FT Business Information Ltd.

The Investment Trust Yearbook, Macmillan.

Taxation

Consumers' Association, *Which? Tax Saving Guide*, 2 Marylebone Road, London NW1 4DX, 1991.

Homer, A., and Burrows, R., *Tolley's Tax Guide*, London: Tolley Publishing Company, 1991.

Sinclair, W. *Allied Dunbar Tax Guide*, Harlow: Longmans, 1991.

Useful Addresses

Association of Futures Brokers and Dealers (AFBD), Stock Exchange Building, Old Broad Street, London EC2N 1EQ.

Association of Investment Trust Companies (AITC), 6th floor, Park House, 16 Finsbury Circus, London EC2M 7JJ.

Bonds and Stock Office, Mythop Road, Marton, Blackpool FY3 9YP, tel. 0253 66151.

Financial Intermediaries, Managers and Brokers Regulatory Association (FIMBRA), Hertsmere House, Hertsmere Road, London E14 4AB.

Life Assurance and Unit Trust Regulatory Organisation (LAUTRO), Centrepoint, 103 New Oxford Street, London WC1A 1QH.

Unit Trust Association, 65 Kingsway, London WC2B 6TD.

Index

By the same author . . .

Get Out of Debt and Prosper

The 10-step plan that really works

- Do you live in dread of quarterly bills?
- Do you have trouble paying off your credit card?
- Are you saddled with mortgage repayments spiralling out of your control?

There are millions of people having serious trouble paying off their debts, and many, many more with some nagging debt they can't quite seem to shake off. If you are one of these people, then *Get Out of Debt and Prosper* could be the answer to your prayers.

In a highly accessible style, Peter Cutler uses self-improvement techniques combined with practical financial advice to help you clear your debts once and for all. Part 1 explains how to:

- Face up to your debts
- Assess what kind of debtor you are
- Use a positive mental attitude to reprogramme your subconscious out of debt-producing habits
- Use meditation to achieve solutions to problems.

Part 2 gives you practical ways to get out of debt, including:

- Simple techniques for recording your spending and analysing the information
- How to negotiate with creditors
- Understanding the complexities of mortgages and how to make them work for you.

Part 3 gives a host of useful ideas and contacts for saving and investment, and tells you how to use the system to your advantage – instead of letting it use you!